Sworn to Silence

A young boy.
An abusive priest.
A buried truth.

BRENDAN BOLAND

With Darragh MacIntyre

EBURY
PRESS

1 3 5 7 9 10 8 6 4 2

First published in 2014 by Ebury Press, an imprint of Ebury Publishing
A Random House Group company

The song lyrics which appear in the text from Bagatelle's 'Trump Card'
and 'Second Violin' are reproduced with kind permission of Liam Reilly.

Author note: I have not named the other children who were with me
on the trips with Fr Brendan Smyth as I have resolved never to reveal
their identities, unless they decide to go public themselves.

Brendan Boland and Darragh MacIntyre have asserted their right
to be identified as the authors of this Work in accordance
with the Copyright, Designs and Patents Act 1988

The Random House Group Limited Reg. No. 954009

Addresses for companies within the Random House Group can be found at
www.randomhouse.co.uk

A CIP catalogue record for this book is available from the British Library

The Random House Group Limited supports the Forest Stewardship
Council® (FSC®), the leading international forest-certification organisation.
Our books carrying the FSC label are printed on FSC®-certified paper. FSC is
the only forest-certification scheme supported by the leading environmental
organisations, including Greenpeace. Our paper procurement policy can be
found at www.randomhouse.co.uk/environment

Printed and bound by CPI Group (UK) Ltd, Croydon, CR0 4YY

ISBN 9780091957469

To buy books by your favourite authors and register for offers visit
www.randomhouse.co.uk

To Martina, my loving and ever supportive wife. My son Niall and his fiancée Sara. To my grandchildren Frankie and Alanna. My father Frank. And especially to the memory of our son Stephen and my mother Anna.

Contents

Chapter 1
First Memories

The abiding memory I have about growing up was that everything was always moving forwards, getting better. There wasn't a lot of money about, but my daddy and mammy always seemed to find enough to provide little extras, like a piano. Now, I am sure it was bought on the never-never, but the point is we managed to have one and most families about didn't have one. Not that you would have felt special about it.

Take the family home. We were reared first in a wee, single-storey house on St Alphonsus Road in Dundalk, County Louth. Then we moved, when I was about five, to a council house in Marian Park across the town.

I remember, to me, it felt like we'd moved into a huge castle. I couldn't believe the size of the bedroom and the wooden floors; it was amazing, absolutely amazing. Of course, it was still only a two-bedroom house. My mother and father had the back room and we had this huge big front room. But not long after we moved in, my father partitioned off our room. He did a proper job, redesigning the landing and fitting two separate doors. There was me – standing beside him doing it – helping him as he was putting the wood in, me there with the hammer. And then I had my own room.

I am the second of four children. The eldest is Anne, then me, followed by Moira and Eilish. My parents, Frank and Anna, were like ourselves – born and bred in Dundalk. Working people. Daddy was from an area called Happy Valley in the town. Great name that! Mammy was from St Alphonsus Road. And that's where we lived first, across the road from where my mother was brought up.

The house backed on to the Rampart River. My earliest memory there was when I was only about two and my father was out in the backyard. He had just stepped out through the wooden door – more a gate – at the end of the yard. There was one step on the other side of this, and then the river. I distinctly remember locking him out, pushing the door shut. The poor man, he couldn't get back in, and was banging at the door, all the while trying to avoid falling into the river.

There was no front garden, only that backyard with an outside toilet. I can still smell it now – not a pong but a very strong whiff of disinfectant. And beside that was a pit that we used for the rubbish, which was cleared out by the council.

You couldn't have called it salubrious, though the house was always spotless. My mother made sure of that, but I know she was as delighted as the rest of us when we moved to Marian Park.

My father had a friend who was on the local council. His name was George Berrills. You had to go through councillors if you needed a house. 'Political patronage' they would call it now. Then it was about sorting out your own. Favours given and favours returned. Lo and behold, we got the house. George was Fianna Fáil, and so my parents voted Fianna Fáil.

* * *

Daddy was working as a compositor at one of the local newspapers, *The Dundalk Democrat*. He was a compositor there for almost all of his working life, setting the type, using hot lead. The smell is what I remember from the times he took me there, the smell of ink, and the men working away, all heads down, concentrating.

His machine was called a linotype – so called because it produced a line of type. Basically, it was like a big typewriter, but one the size of a porch and with 90 characters. Most newspapers used this technology right up until the last thirty years. His was a skilled job and in Dundalk, at the time, considered well paid.

I know he started at 10 shillings a week, as an apprentice, back in 1939. Seven years later – that's how long it took to serve his time – he was put on proper wages: £4 and 10 shillings. Big wages in 1946.

Daddy was a good father, a great father. He had a face that was always ready to smile, a big open-faced smile. Not tall by any description, but I wouldn't have called him small either. Not the way I saw him. If he was a footballer, you'd say he had a 'neat' build. And that's another thing. He was always well turned out but he wasn't fastidious about it.

I just remember him coming in from work and he'd have marbles for me. He would always bring in a little present: a little dinky car or boxes of marbles. Then he would play a game. He would hide the present, maybe behind the sofa, or underneath the oil cloth that we had then, not carpet. The big clue would be the hump of the oil cloth. Away you would go and retrieve it from underneath.

He and my mother met at a dance. They went out with each other for eighteen months; he could not wait to marry her. That was 1953. I have a picture of them cutting their wedding cake. The pair of them are beaming, in a pose which is more natural than any such photos I have seen. You see the joy in the moment. They look happy and excited and set for a great voyage.

Mammy was a total lady. A lovely, kind woman. She was never inclined to fuss too much but was always ready to deliver a good word. She had worked before they married, in Halliday's shoe factory. An uncle and an aunt were there too.

* * *

It's hard to imagine now, but Dundalk was a thriving place in the 1960s. A town of about 20,000. You had the army barracks, Louth County Hospital and lots of industry. Halliday's would become Clarks shoes, and there was a time when the guts of 1,000 people were employed there. You had two breweries, Harp and Macardles. And then there was Carroll's, the cigarette manufacturers. Work was not in short supply.

There were other advantages with those particular factories in the town. The shoe factories offered discounts for staff. Carroll's had, what was called, a staff issue – might have been as much as sixty fags each – and there was a free drink allowance from the breweries too.

Cars must have been the first sign of prosperity. We didn't have one, but more and more started to appear on the estate, and on the roads about the town. Daddy relied on the bike for years after. On Friday nights, it was used to carry home the ultimate treat – fish and chips. He'd come home with the bags of fish and chips stuffed up his jumper to keep them warm.

Often he'd take us with him on the crossbar. That was craic, freewheeling and chatting, almost smothered by his flapping coat. Sounds dangerous now, but I'm sure I never felt as safe as I did sitting on that crossbar, all wrapped up by Daddy.

Cousins were carried on that bike. Even my aunts. A proper all-purpose vehicle. Mammy tried to get in on the act too. I came across her being taught how to ride a bike one day. An aunt was holding the bike and Mammy was on the saddle, terrified. She got all embarrassed and asked me not to tell Daddy – she wanted it to be a surprise for him.

The extended family was important then. Daddy's parents died when I was very young, but my mother's parents were central in my life and I spent lots of time with them. My Aunt Bridie, who was the only member of the family with a car, used to drive my grandmother and grandfather and me to Arklow, in County Wicklow, for weekends. She sat with the seat right up to the steering wheel and never came out of second gear. I remember Mammy being thrilled when Aunt Bridie, who never married, moved with my grandparents to a house around the corner from our home. She was like a second mum to me.

Those journeys to Arklow, where my grandfather was born, were always eventful, not so much the actual stays there but the journeys themselves. My grandfather was the original back-seat driver, saying, 'Bridie, slow down. Watch this bad bend. Mind this car coming towards us.' And all the while she couldn't have been doing more than 40mph.

When we got there, we would stay in an area called Ferrybank, with family and friends of my grandparents, so I would just sit there for the weekend listening to their conversation with the odd trip to the shops like Dunnes Stores to brighten up my life. They would always buy me new clothes and maybe some sweets. I loved them dearly and I know they loved me too, but I dreaded the driving on the way home.

My grandfather and I were really, really close. When my granny, my mother and my Aunt Bridie used to go shopping, I would go round and I would sit with my grandfather and we would watch television.

He was a big strong man. As long as I knew him, he had a shock of white hair on top of a face which had a very gentle almost slightly quizzical look about it. You hear about kids and their relationship with their grandparents; well, mine was straight out of the story books. I loved him dearly and I know he loved me too.

We used to watch the wrestling, on a Saturday morning. Mick McManus was the big baddie back then. The pair of us would sit together and follow sport through the day. We were so close; he used to come round here and just talk to me. Later, he kick-started my career by getting me a job in the place where he had worked.

* * *

There was never a cross word in the house. I actually can't remember one argument between the parents, not one. If they had their differences, and I'm not sure they had, they had them out of earshot of us. Another thing, I was never slapped by either of them, nor were the girls. Now that, I think, was unusual. I could be told off right enough but not beaten. Never. And it was Daddy who did the chastising if it had to be done. The classic one was my mother saying, 'Wait 'til your father gets home.'

I know what other lads went through, beaten black and blue, I know some of them were, but with Daddy it was just a telling-off. The worst time – I'll never forget it – concerned a friend of mine and money.

I was out playing that day with this friend – I'll call him 'Jack', to spare him embarrassment now – and he goes: 'I've got a secret.'

'What's that?' I says.

'Come and I will show you.'

So we went up and there was a house on the corner with a big hedge, and there was a rock in the hedge and he pulled the rock away, and there was this bundle of money. There must have been £50 in it; that was a lot of money.

I said to him: 'Where did you get that?'

And he said his granny gave it to him.

So that was all right. We put it back and we went to the shop and we bought sweets, and we bought a packet of fags. We bought Sweet Afton. I knew if I went to the shop and bought Sweet Afton the shop-keeper would think they were for my father, because he smoked Afton.

Later on that day, or the next day, I was going back up to the house on the corner to get some money for sweets for myself. There I was buried in the hedge, hoking about for the money, when my father caught me. He sees the money and asks where on earth I got it from.

'It's not mine; it's Jack's.'

He says, 'And where did Jack get it?'

I immediately answered, 'From his granny.'

But Daddy wasn't having it, so he called round to Jack's house. And what does this lad do but blame me.

Jack said I robbed a garage. The story he told was true, except that I had no part in it. There was a petrol station on the way home from school and Jack had gone in when the cashier wasn't looking and stuffed his pockets with the contents of the till.

This was probably the first time my father ever heard me curse. I swore at Jack. And he kept on insisting that I did it. My father looked like he believed Jack, so I kept on, 'No! It wasn't me, Daddy. I swear it wasn't me.'

Eventually my father said, 'I am taking you up to the Garda barracks.' He put me on the crossbar of the bike. All the way up there, I was crying and going 'It wasn't me'. We got to the barracks – right up to the door – and I was still protesting my innocence.

That's the point when my father finally believed me. He took me home and went off to speak to Jack's parents. They had to pay back the money to the petrol station. I ended up being cleared, but it was awful. It was a nightmare, you know, for that lad to blame me, and then for my father not to believe me. I don't blame my father now. Looking back, he caught me putting my hand in the hedge, getting the money. And even then, he didn't strike me.

I suppose you would describe him as even-tempered. Others probably thought of him as a mild-mannered man, which he is. No bad habits, but he did like the horses. I'm sure he lost a couple of bob over the years, but I mostly remember the winnings. He would tell us stories about when he used to win. And when he did, he would be very generous. If someone needed a bit of cash and he had some, he wouldn't be slow in getting it to them. Off on his bike with his pockets bulging. I know that.

My mammy, Anna, never made an issue of it. She hated any sort of conflict. And I know she and my father loved each other. There were no big demonstrations of it in our company and they certainly didn't blow money on big nights out together. That wasn't their style. Neither drank. So out to the pub wasn't their scene or a restaurant either.

But I always felt their love for each other just the same. Unspoken. Even with us, it wasn't kisses and cuddles. Obviously, they were from a different era, passing on what they had learned from their own parents. And yet they made it clear that the family, the children, were their number one priority. As far as they were both concerned, we had a nice family cocoon and so long as that was protected, all was well.

* * *

Family values and the Church were all as one with them. If we were sitting watching the television and a movie came on with people kissing, my mother would say, 'Turn that over.' They might have been stricter than some families in that regard, but back then it seemed very normal.

Religion was a major matter in the home: grace before meals and the Rosary, faithfully, every night. Come six o'clock, the Angelus would come on the television. You had to be quiet for the Angelus, the bells ringing from the TV set. Then onto your knees. All of us. Five decades of the Rosary. An eternity for a child. Often we'd all be there, gathered around the floor, scattered between the chairs, and then one of us would start giggling. Of course giggles are infectious.

First Anne would lose it, then me, and before long the lot of us children were laughing. If this was spotted, we would have to start from the beginning. Children are quick learners, though, so we got to the stage where we made sure not to laugh. Did I know what any of this was about? No. I knew enough to realise that it was about God, but that was it. Sure, what did any child know? But it was important for my parents.

I don't imagine many young families today do the Rosary. In fact, it might be considered odd behaviour. Nor would many young families have their house decorated with the sort of religious paraphernalia and assorted icons that my parents' home boasted. At best, you'd think them eccentric.

There were religious pictures and ornaments in every room. We had a lamp of the Sacred Heart and a holy water font by the front door. A picture of the Mother of Perpetual Succour, a portrait of Christ on the cross and a picture of the Pope – Pope John it was then – hanging inside. There was an array of other bits and pieces: statues of the Virgin Mary, Lourdes memorabilia and a crucifix in a glass globe.

But that wasn't unusual then. Most houses about would have been the same. Except, I suppose, for Protestant homes and we didn't go into those.

As a child I was afraid of Protestants. Don't ask me to explain rationally why I was afraid of Protestants, but I was. There was one man called Isaac Dunne. We knew he was Protestant and he lived around the corner. Whenever we saw him about, we would run, scarper for the hills, all of us kids. What I knew about Protestants was simple enough: they didn't believe in God, they don't go to Mass, they didn't believe in Mary the Mother of God. They weren't true Christians. They were dark people; they walked on the dark side. It's crazy, but that was the image you had.

In fact, Isaac Dunne was a lovely man. Once you got to know him, you found that he was one of the finest men about. Later, he helped my father run a senior citizens club.

It's really only looking back that I understand how much of a role religion played in my childhood. Even though I didn't see it as great fun, I didn't see it as a wholly negative thing either. It was simply what you did.

* * *

As for my parents, I don't think you could define them by just saying they were religion mad. There was much more to them. My father was really community-focused. He was involved in setting up the Marian Park

Residents' Association. He worked with a senior citizens club, organised sports days, and he ran a football team.

It was because of him that I got to play at Croke Park, the headquarters of the Gaelic Athletic Association (GAA), the equivalent of Wembley for soccer. It was most lads' dream to play there and he made sure I got there.

He helped organise the street leagues round Dundalk. There was Seatown and Fatima, and a host of other areas, plus, of course, Marian Park. Now, I am not sure how exactly it worked, but he had put together a Dundalk selection to play a team from Dublin – Marino, I think – in Croke Park in a special one-off game.

I knew it was special to play at 'Croker'. The stadium was no ordinary venue. It was vast, especially to me as a child. The famous Hogan Stand loomed over one side of the pitch. Even then, I knew that it had been named after Michael Hogan, a footballer from Tipperary who had been killed on Bloody Sunday, 21 November 1920. Hogan had been playing that day when British soldiers raided the sports ground, looking for IRA men who had killed intelligence officers in overnight attacks in Dublin. The soldiers opened fire on the crowd, killing 14 people.

Another section of the stadium has a terrace called Hill 16, so called because it was built using rubble from some of the destroyed buildings of Dublin after the Easter Rising of 1916. Primary school was big on history when I was there.

As to the football itself, I know that I was useless and no one would have selected me to play. My father was just trying to give me my moment of glory, pushing me forward, saying, 'Yes, he's on.'

The team was picked and we went out and the opposition came out. We felt like little dwarves compared to them. Some of them even had beards. We got hammered, really taught a lesson. Not that there was any point in me learning anything because I had no concept of what I was supposed to do, where I was meant to be. To me, Gaelic football was just about catching the ball and kicking it, neither of which I was terribly accomplished at.

In fairness, my daddy wasn't one of those who would shout at their child during a game. He knew it was enough that I ran about on Croke Park. Daddy was child-centred before the term was invented.

Holidays were always taken in Greenore, a port village about fifteen miles north-east of Dundalk. Back in the day, it was a thriving resort town, with its own railway line and a smashing hotel. But by the time we were going, it was really only for daytrippers and determined holidaymakers like ourselves.

Every summer, John Carter, who used to sell vegetables at the Square in Dundalk and had a Volkswagen van, would give us all a lift to Greenore. Mammy and Daddy would be squeezed into the front of the van, with us kids sitting on crates in the back. Away we went for two weeks.

We stayed in what I used to think were fishing huts but they were actually beach huts, like you still see in England. There was just the one room, but we had beds and a sink and a sort of a sitting room, more space inside than you'd think.

Greenore was so special to us. You could stand there on the beach and look across Carlingford Lough to the Mourne Mountains in County Down. The Mournes were only a couple of miles away, but in my mind's eye they were part of a magical wonderland of mystery, with forest-covered slopes and peaks and valleys, rolling away on the northern horizon.

Directly to the east lay the Irish Sea and the Isle of Man, which I was certain could be seen on a clear day, and beyond that, England and Liverpool. When I got half a chance, I would sneak off to the harbour and watch the ships come and go. As harbours go, it wasn't particularly impressive, with just one long pier, but it had a very beautiful lighthouse.

The lighthouse's outstanding feature was its size. It was pint-sized, compared with most, not much bigger than a two-storey house. But it was very pretty, all white and red, with an intricate framed glass globe on top. Night after night, its beam would sweep around the docks, almost catching our abode on the shore before it finally reached out to sea. The building is there yet, but the lights are long extinguished.

The beach was our main playground. I never learned to swim, despite the best attempts of my parents, but I could have paddled for Ireland. We were hardy enough when I think about it. The water was never anything other than cold, but away we would go, up to our waists in it, goose pimples aflame, having persuaded ourselves that this was just about as much fun as children could have. Mammy would keep watch, but I have no memory of her ever going to the sea. My father, on the other hand, was a brilliant swimmer and would swim great distances from the beach but spent most of his time chasing us through the surf.

There was fishing there too. Mackerel. Me and Daddy at the pier and on the shore casting into shoals of fish. August was the best time. We'd land buckets of them, share them around the other families, and whatever was left Mammy would cook up for us. Sweet and delicious. Cockles were another treat. We could go searching for them at low tide, looking for a tell-tale lump in the sand with a whirly top and then dig ferociously for them. Delicious.

There was no shortage of entertainment because we provided it. The four of us children were organised by my father. Anne, my eldest sister, was a great singer. We would then put on these shows for others staying around about. There were the Websters, who stayed in a fancy old train carriage, and the McGrains, who were close by. Lots of kids from Marian Park would be down visiting too.

We would rehearse the show all day, singing and dancing, using tennis racquets as guitars and then, in the evenings, we would perform in front of all these people.

The four of us, the Boland group.

'One banana, two banana. Three banana, four …'

Remember the Banana Splits? We used to do that.

'Three wheels on my wagon and I'm still rolling along …'

This was taken very seriously by us. We'd act out the songs as well. Great fun. And appreciated by our audience too.

Sometimes there was also pure unadulterated manic excitement. The older brother of a friend of mine owned a big Honda motorbike and would take me for spins around Greenore on the back of it. A Gold Wing, 1000 cc, ten times the size of little me. There I'd go, no helmet, perched up on the back, holding on for dear life. It was an adrenaline rush before I ever knew the word. I'm not sure if my parents would have approved, but it was fantastic. And yes, mad!

Chapter 2
School Days

First Communion was a big step for me, in my wee suit jacket and short trousers with zip pockets. As far as I was concerned, I was now a grown-up member of God's family. This was a serious matter. I was taught how to receive the host properly and, of course, what to do at Confession. Sin? I had to learn what was a sin and what wasn't.

I always had the same sins every week:

'Cursing. Telling fibs. I was bold to my mammy and daddy.'

The day itself there was a big fuss. Up I went in fear and dread of making a disgrace of myself. The Communion breakfast came afterwards and then the most unholy task of gathering the financial award due to me for reaching this stage of my young Catholic life. Aunts, uncles, the grandparents, thrusting notes and coins at me. I thought the whole thing a fine tradition.

I can't remember my total, but I do know that others would boast about how much they had got. I was in no doubt that I had just reached a major milestone.

You could set the clock by God in our house. Come Saturday night, seven o'clock, bath time. Then Sunday morning up early for ten o'clock mass. I had to put on my Sunday clothes, all to make sure I was looking the best for mass. Even as a child, everything had to be proper: tie, proper jumper, hair perfectly combed. The best of outfits was kept for Easter.

We would leave in good time and walk the half mile or so to the Redeemer Church. We'd go with neighbours, the Morgan and the Quinliven families. We'd meet on the road and head on up to this brand new church.

It is one of those post-Vatican Two Catholic churches, semi-circular, very modern design, very bright and very big. As a child, it looked completely enormous – this house of God – for a very big man, I thought. I didn't look forward to going to mass. Most children didn't, I am sure. For me it was a chore, not any worse than that, but certainly not a fun-filled activity, no matter how holy it was.

Sunday evening, at 6 o'clock, meant Benediction. This was another date on the weekly calendar that you had no choice about. It involved the whole family, plus my grandparents and my aunt. Oddly perhaps, to me this was more interesting than the Sunday mass. It was a full-blooded ritual, with the scent of incense in the air and the prayers delivered in a kind of chanting rhythm.

There was plenty of ritual. Monday nights brought the novena in the church. Again, the whole family was present, and there were prayers: 'Blessed Oliver, pray for us'. The priest would talk and say something and everybody would answer back. More chants, that's the way I looked at it. The only drama would be the fear of the giggles again. Worse than laughing in the home during the Rosary was the prospect of laughing in a public place when all around are straight-faced and solemn.

Myself and my sister used to be sitting giggling and laughing. Pray for us, pray for us. And my mother and father would look at us every time. Not happy. If they ever really got upset with us, it was about the giggles.

* * *

One of the fringe benefits of getting to the age of Confession was that I seemed to be taken more seriously, in religious terms. Before long I was allowed to go to the Redemptorist Missions. These were real highlights locally and starred preachers from the

Redemptorist Order who would visit towns around Ireland and hold prayer gatherings for days and weeks at a time. Sometimes it involved real fire and brimstone stuff.

I wasn't allowed to go in the early days; I was considered to be too young, because apparently the priests would speak about sex at some of them. The men went one night, the women another.

I can't remember exactly what age I was, but my father thought I was old enough and took me along and it was a great feeling to be allowed to go to the missions with my father. My mother would say, 'You are going with Daddy, it will be great.'

And actually you would go and it was a bit of a laugh. It wasn't like going to mass, where you were afraid to look at the priest crooked and you were answering for the sake of answering. At this mission the priest was actually talking to you and it wasn't really religious. At least, it wasn't like most of my experience of religion, which involved something that had to be endured. I enjoyed it, because the priest would be frank and laughing and telling jokes in the pulpit, totally different to mass.

Most of my friends then would have come from families that were already known or close to my parents. The religion that I saw and practised in my home was more or less the same for most of them too.

Our faith was taken for granted. It was never discussed or analysed. I can't remember any talk about the importance of God or why we were doing such and such. It was just the way most of us lived our lives. Now, I realise that even in the Ireland of those times, forty, fifty years ago, we were probably more conservative, maybe more devout, than others, but we certainly didn't stand out. As a child, it was much more a marker of my path through life than it was a conscious way of life.

Then came the call for altar boys. This was through school. The teachers said they were taking in altar boys. 'Did anyone want to go?' So, I volunteered.

Brother Ultan did the training. Now, to my young mind, there was a lot to learn, but it was fun doing it with all the other boys from school. I think we got an hour a week for instruction, which was good because it meant you were out of the classroom.

I actually got a transfer from the church where I'd trained, which was on one side of the town, to my home parish of the Holy Redeemer. The job itself was, in my opinion then, a very responsible one. The entire congregation was waiting for you to ring the bell to give them the signal that the next stage of the mass is coming and communion was on its way.

You would listen intently to the mass to make sure you heard the cue words, then a twist of the wrist and you'd ring the bells. If you got it wrong, well, that might be a serious sin. Concentration was key. This was scary betimes because the priest, though nice enough, could be very strict.

Of course, you mightn't get the job of ringing the bell, which reduced the excitement and gave you less of a role in the whole affair. And the other trial was going around holding the communion plate under people's chins. That was another scary one, in case you missed somebody's blessed host. And there was the prospect of being damned to Hell if you dropped it. All of these fears played out in my head, but my hand was sure.

There was a part of me then that felt I was almost in training to be a priest myself. I believed the work I was doing on the altar was God's work. My family, I'm sure, was very proud of me, up there helping out. And I knew my grandmother had high hopes of me.

She used to say she always wanted her son, Michael, to be a priest, so I would say to myself, 'I will make my grandmother proud. I will be a priest myself.'

I'm sure I wasn't the first child to think of the priesthood at that time. It seems absurd looking back, but the only priests I knew, to this point, were kind, genial characters. When they were nice to you, it was like being blessed by God himself.

They were impressive, too, and I suppose I was in awe of the way they were held in such high regard. You noticed things. There was a clear deference to them, which, at the time, meant that they were important people. Though, I'm not sure if I thought of them as 'people'. It was drummed into you that they were God's emissaries on earth, so not really people. They were somehow 'other', better than the rest of us.

I would overhear the odd remarks among the family, suggesting that I might make a fine priest, and I am sure I smiled away. I know they were half in jest, but I took it seriously enough. You were left in no doubt that if you chose that path, the family would be roaring you on, my grandmother leading the charge. And for a while, I gave it thought – well, the sort of throw-away thought a child might give to it. Perhaps, fortunately, it never fully formed in my mind because I don't imagine I would have been a brilliant priest.

* * *

I enjoyed school, mostly. The De La Salle Primary School. I have no horror stories about the religious there. It was quite civilised by the standards of the time. This was the era when I became interested in music. It started when Brother Martin (we called him 'Fuzzy' because of his hair) came into class and asked if anybody wanted to have trials for the De La Salle accordion band. As usual, I volunteered and had to stay back the next day, after school, for lessons. After a few lessons, he must have thought that I had potential because he sent a note home to my parents. The next thing I remember, an accordion appeared. We had band practice once a week and, before long, I was just about good enough to join the big boys in the band. We played at a lot of different events, from school concerts to Easter parades. I remember one year playing on a float in the May-time festival parade. It was very embarrassing because we had to wear a kilt as part of the uniform and we were sitting down. Even then, I didn't think it was a good look.

The accordion has its own special place in my history.

I can boast of winning the County Louth championship for accordion. I was playing under ten, but there were only two of us in the competition. I started playing and then I stopped. I'd made a mistake – it was the nerves. After that, I started and stopped, and I started again. One mistake followed another. But I won, so the other bloke must have been absolutely woeful. I still have that medal.

Mammy, of course, thought I was a virtuoso. Every time anybody came to the house, she would say, 'Brendan, play the accordion. Brendan, play the accordion.'

I was shy, not very good at it anyway, and I didn't want to play it, so I would say, 'What will I play?' That was my stalling tactic.

One day, she said to me, 'If you say that to me once more, I will hit you with something.' Of course I repeated the question. Next thing, she fires a polish brush at me and the polish brush hits the accordion – Bang! And she has put a dent in it. It was weird to see it happen. That was the only time my mother ever lifted her hand or raised a finger. I can't say I liked that instrument.

I had no shortage of friends, but at this time was probably closer to my sister Anne than anyone. We were thick as thieves, the two of us. I remember one night we decided to rap doors and run away. We got to our corner and rapped a neighbour's door and ran like hell, only to run into my mother. She inquired why we were running and we said we wanted to get home quick. Just then, the neighbour came round the corner and told my mother what we had done. Mammy was mortified. She told us she was going to kill us and tell my father when she got back, but all she did later was give us a stern look. She never said another word about it.

I did kick about with a bunch of friends after school, playing on the wee green in front of the house. Smoking was about the boldest thing I did. I was about nine years old when I had my first one.

Coming home from school there was a shop where you could buy singles. 2p for a Major and 1 and a half pence for Carroll's. I'd get a Major (they were the strongest of the filtered fags) and a packet of crisps. The crisps would take the smell away, or so we thought. Remember our age, nine years old, and the shopkeeper selling them loose to us children, knowing we were going to smoke them. They'd be arrested on the spot today.

I smoked them more than once at a place called Cúchulainn's Castle, a magical place. It's just a few hundred yards away from my home place, close to the Castletown Road, on the edge of the town. We'd escape there on weekends and play hard among the trees on the slopes of the ancient, circular earthen ramparts. Within the ramparts stood, what I thought to be, an old castle. Back then, I assumed the castle had been built by Cúchulainn, the mythical Irish hero. In fact, the stone castle is an eighteenth-century tower, a folly built by a wealthy Dundalk merchant. But the ramparts date back to the twelfth or thirteenth century, when a Norman motte and bailey was constructed on the site. No matter, we were happy playing at being in Na Fianna, the legendary band of Irish warriors, who were said to protect the old Irish High Kings.

Close to the castle was the Dundalk Rugby Club. That managed to keep me occupied on a regular Saturday through the winters. We could run around and mess with our friends there, and then in with me to the clubhouse, where I would invariably find my father's brother, my Uncle Paddy, and my Auntie Bridie. Paddy was the physio for the rugby team for many years and Bridie did the catering for the teams on match days. They would welcome me and my friends into the club and were always generous with soft drinks; we called them 'minerals' and dozens of packets of crisps. Then off to the sink with us to help with the washing-up. One of those great trade-offs children specialise in. Paddy lived almost forever, dying in January 2013 at the age of ninety-three.

Come high summer, there was another castle to occupy. A two-hour walk took us the seven miles to

Castle Roche to the north-west of Dundalk. Now, there is no mistaking this for anything other than a fortress built in times when danger lurked in the surrounding bogs and woods. Its thick walls still straddle the rock it was built on, beside what was once the main route north into wild Ulster. It is a Norman ruin, built in the thirteenth century by Rohesia de Verdun. The story is told that this lass had a bad temper and had a problem finding a partner, but she had lots of land and ambitions for a strong castle, so she promised her hand and her wealth to the man who could build her the castle.

Sure enough, a man was found. He obliged with the stonework and the couple married in great style. But after the wedding banquet in the brand new castle, Rohesia enticed the lad to their chambers and suggested he look on their great estate from a window. One push was all it took for the opening to be rechristened the 'Murder Window'. The Norman temptress kept her wealth.

I'd head to Castle Roche with the Finnegan brothers on Sunday afternoons and we'd set about defending Leinster from the Ulster invaders. Or cowboys and Indians. When our imaginations tired, we'd make for the Finnegans' Aunt Betty's farmhouse nearby. We would help her get the cows ready for milking, rounding them up and herding them into the yard. Afterwards, she'd feed us up and drive us home, a fair deal and, as I say, us kids were good at those deals.

We were all kept on a reasonably loose set of reins, but you knew there were rules.

The most important rule was that whoever got home from school first got the skin of the custard.

* * *

Our schools were close by, so we got home each lunch-time for our dinner. Once you hit the gate, you'd call out to Mammy and hope you were the first of the kids to land. Mince and spuds was the staple meal, always a stew on Saturday, followed by homemade custard.

That was the dinner routine at home. Daddy would come for his own dinner at two. In the evenings, it was just a light supper of tea and toast, sometimes banana sandwiches. Bedtime was milk and biscuits, and a piggyback up the stairs from Daddy. He would tell stories too, made-up yarns and adventures with each of us as the central characters.

Neither of my parents drank alcohol. Both were lifelong teetotal. They were pioneers, badged members of the Pioneer Total Abstinence Association of the Sacred Heart, a Catholic-based temperance association, which despite Ireland's association with alcohol or because of it, had thousands of members across the country.

In due course, I became a pioneer myself, encouraged by the parents. I had to take the pledge, promising to abstain from booze, and I received a nice wee pin for my efforts. It was simply the way I was brought up, and it seemed a logical step, though I would choose to drink when I was a teenager.

At the time, I thought it was odd when people were drunk or I got the smell of alcohol off someone's breath. The strangest thing was seeing people drunk in public. And my parents left me in no doubt that it was a bad thing.

Occasionally, there would be a fellow coming home, after a day's drinking, straggling up the Castletown Road and into Marian Park, and my mother would look over and remark, half to herself, 'There's your man and he's drunk again.'

There was one fella; he would be coming home and he wouldn't know where he was. He used to get out of the car in the middle of the street and think he was home. And then he'd stagger across the road, looking first at one house and then another, completely lost and blind drunk.

There was also an awareness of the violence that can spill out of drink. I know my father intervened once to protect a woman and her family from an abusive and drunken husband. Daddy restrained him and kept the woman and her children safe, so I don't think it was just piety that shaped their attitude to drink; they knew the worst effects of it.

* * *

The town was starting to change by the start of the 1970s. The Troubles were underway up north. I had no understanding of them, but suddenly there were Northern accents around. Hundreds of families moved south across the border, all Catholics, to Dundalk. Many of them were refugees from Belfast and places like that which were under pressure. Others had, I know now, family in the IRA, and they were effectively on the run here just over the border.

I remember when the Troubles really took off. We were watching television at home between throwing snowballs the night of Bloody Sunday in Derry. The sight I won't forget is that priest – later Bishop Edward Daly – waving the white handkerchief. Snow had arrived that evening. I was outside playing in the snow and running in and out to get warm, finding the grown-ups crowded around the TV, watching news flashes as the death toll kept rising.

Generally though the Troubles didn't register too much in the home. Mammy and Daddy were clear that Ian Paisley was a troublemaker, but, other than that, they weren't very involved.

Mammy would go, 'Here is that Paisley *git.*' She used to call him a git. 'Do you hear him? Frank, do you hear him?'

They would be excited watching the news and sometimes upset, but it wasn't a very political household. There was enough going on without that.

Then came the big housing development Muirhevnamor, a brand new estate across the town. It seemed huge to me. One minute there were green fields, the next a small town. 'Little Belfast' we called it. In time, Dundalk itself got the nickname 'El Paso' as there were so many Northerners about. It was a puzzle to me, the whole thing. But I felt certain, as I am sure most of the town did, that the Nationalists, that is the Catholics, were being hard done by and that the Unionists and the British government were responsible.

Chapter 3
First Encounter

It was the summer of 1973. I was off on school holidays but still serving mass at the Redeemer Church every Sunday morning and then helping at Sunday evening Benediction. There was a noticeboard in the church detailing any weddings or christenings coming up. We could choose which ones we wanted to do. We used to want to do weddings because you would get money for it. The couple getting married would give an envelope for the altar boys.

We were given this task to do, this wedding on a Friday morning at 11. It was a couple I didn't know and it was presided over by a priest I had never met. We set up the mass and went through the whole lot. Afterwards, we were standing outside, myself and another altar boy – I can't remember who it was – and the priest came out and he started chatting to us.

He was doing small talk but he seemed very nice. He chatted away to the pair of us and then asked us where we lived. I told him I was from quite close. And then he asked if I knew anywhere he could get a cup of tea, so I said, 'Yes. Sure come down to my house. I am sure my mammy would make a cup of tea for you.'

Now a lot of people have this image of Fr Brendan Smyth as a very ugly, awful man. It is as if his looks matched the terrible things he did. But to me he looked completely normal. In fact, he appeared to be a lovely man, a gentleman, who even in the course of a few minutes of small chat seemed to take a genuine interest in me. He could have been described as handsome, I suppose. Tall and broad-shouldered and fond of laughing. What's not to like?

He offered me a lift home, which seemed a reasonable trade-off. I was certain that Mammy would be delighted to see a priest coming in with me. Whenever a local priest called she would make such a fuss over him. I would never have asked any ordinary stranger in for tea, but I knew she would be thrilled with the prospect of a priest visiting, granting her his presence. Intuitively, I knew it was all the more significant because Fr Smyth wasn't from our parish.

He sat down and he had tea and chatted. He was there for quite a while because I remember my father coming home from work. He introduced himself as Fr Brendan Smyth, a member of the Norbertine Order from Kilnacrott Abbey in County Cavan. He had fundraising literature for his order with him and he showed that to Mammy and Daddy. They seemed impressed with him too. I know my father was every bit as delighted as Mammy. Before Fr Smyth left, there was a bit of horse play with me and my sisters, tickling and playing with us. Fun and games.

* * *

Fr Smyth began a pattern of visits. Once a week, or every fortnight, he'd land and stay for hours every time.

He was never in any rush and would play with us and chat to my parents. His car was always stocked with sweets. Every time he would come, he'd knock on the door and then say to me, 'Brendan, come out to the car 'til you see what I have for you.'

Out I would go; he'd open the boot and it was like an Aladdin's cave of sugary treats.

He'd have Mars bars, Kit Kats and various mixtures of sweets, like Fruit Salads and Black Jacks. He would dole them out to us, and any kids that were on the street, passing by, would get some too. And for me that was all positive, great. All my little friends were getting sweets because of me, so I felt good.

He was like the Pied Piper with those sweets. Later, I learned that he got the sweets through his role running a school tuck shop at St Norbert's College, which was managed by the Norbertines at Kilnacrott. That makes sense because the sweets were packed and boxed like you might buy them in a wholesaler.

His visits became part of the family routine. He would hang out with my mammy and daddy. By then, they were helping raise funds for the Norbertines; he would leave collection envelopes with them to pass around and try to get some cash for their mission. Then he would play with us, me and my sisters: sitting us on his knee, tickling and running after you. You would fall on the floor and he would chase you, pull you up and back on his knees. It seemed totally harmless and was new to us because that wasn't Daddy's style.

He quickly became a sort of uncle, embedded in our family. And it wasn't just our house he visited. He would call to my grandparents, who lived around the corner. The visits were arranged in advance, so we always knew when he was coming, the exact time and day he would arrive. I know that my parents considered him a close friend and looked forward to him coming as much as we did.

My father has told me that he thought the friendship with Fr Smyth was the start of me taking a serious interest in the priesthood, which would have been a really great thing as far as he and Mammy were concerned. Me, I was like any child, happy to be spoilt by this nice man.

There was nothing too odd about anything for some time. Even when I started to go away in the car with him. He would call for me in the evening and take me out the Greenore Road to the Mount Oliver Religious Institute. This was run by the Franciscan Order of nuns and he would say mass there. I would do altar boy duty. Afterwards, Fr Smyth would come back to our home and stay for a few hours and have a cup of tea or two.

Years later, I came to understand what he was doing. He was grooming us, all of us – my parents, my sisters and, of course, me. It was classic paedophile behaviour; it was impossible to imagine anything untoward happening in this man's presence. He had our complete trust. Worse than that, we were all keen to please him. It was easy to see why as he showered us with sweets and that little bit of extra attention that made us all feel special, in some indefinable way.

My parents, too, were in his trap. As good, God-fearing, righteous people, they felt that they had been chosen to be bestowed with the sanctified gift of Fr Smyth's visits. They mightn't have admitted it to themselves, but I know they must have quietly revelled in his attention, just like us children. Not too many of our neighbours in Marian Park had a priest calling to the door.

* * *

It must have been a year or so after I first met Fr Smyth that he came round to the house one day and put what I thought was a brilliant proposition to my parents. He told my father that he was taking a few children down on a trip to Cork and he asked if he could take me along, and Daddy said, 'Yes, no bother.'

Remember the furthest I had ever got from Dundalk was to nearby Greenore, though there had been the occasional day trip with the school and, once or twice, with the family to Mosney holiday camp, our very own Butlins. But that was also just down the road. I had been to Arklow, in County Wicklow, but that was on one of those wrenching family drives.

Cork, well, that was the other end of the country. There was one local family who managed to go to

Europe, to Spain I think, and they came back each summer all bronzed. To me that summer, Cork was every bit as exotic as Spain.

I was now eleven years old, starting to get obsessed with music since I realised I was never going to play for County Louth at Croke Park or anywhere else for that matter. The piano had landed at this stage. It was no Steinway but it had pride of place in our home. Anne was terribly musical and she was encouraged by Mammy and Daddy. She took lessons and so did I.

Once I saw that Anne was learning quickly, I thought I'd have a go. I was already able to play the piano accordion, which was half the battle. All I had to do was learn the left-hand part. Our teacher, Kathleen Duffy, was such a good instructor she had me playing 'Greensleeves' with both hands in no time at all; I was so proud of myself.

But my music interests were being shaped elsewhere, by the pop charts and, after that, by the very best of glam rock, Slade. They had what I thought then was a fantastic song up at number one that year: 'Mama Weer All Crazee Now'. I was a fan, like everyone, of *Top of the Pops*. The mad thing was, like most of the kids around, we had all the UK TV channels at home.

My father started running hops. He'd run hops on Sundays for the children in Marian Park, him and a man called Barney Morgan. They were held in a community hall, now a boxing club. Sunday afternoon for the young ones, which was my age group, and then on a Sunday night he'd have a hop for the teenagers. I'd pressurise him to be allowed to go to the teenage hops, but it was no-go.

'If I let you in, I have to let all the other kids in.'

The thing is, he didn't just organise the hops – he was the DJ too. Himself and Barney, working the racks. Funny to think about it. Every time I imagine I have my father in a box, he goes and does something like that. Same all the years. He'd go to the record shop in the town centre and arrive back with that week's chart toppers: Gary Glitter, Bay City Rollers, T Rex, Rod Stewart and the Rubettes. The best thing was he'd keep them at home, so I would get to listen to them to my heart's content.

I was such an innocent lad. Smoking the odd fag was the worst thing I did. And even then, I would end up trying to hide the fact that they set me off coughing.

The bootboy look was cool then: Doc Marten boots, stripped socks, parallels, denim or leather jacket and long hair completed the outfit. Me, well, I just made for cover when they came along. They were older and one hundred per cent tougher than me. It wasn't that I was a weakling but I had no interest in fighting. Watching *Hawaii Five-O* or *Dr Who* was the closest I got to confrontation.

I had no notion that my life was about to be changed forever. But it wasn't just me. Looking back, that was same year we joined the European Common Market. Decimalisation had happened a little earlier. We were told great things about what the EEC would bring to us, but I am not sure if it did my town any good. The local industries would all start to feel the pressure of competing in a common market. Jobs would never be as plentiful. I think it rained a lot that summer too.

But the deluge of an Irish summer didn't dampen the prospects of the trip to Cork. I'd get to see the entire country, make new friends and listen to music. Fr Smyth had an eight-track tape player in the car. From memory, he played mostly music from the Beatles, which suited me entirely, though it wasn't glam rock.

* * *

The day of the trip dawned. It was a mid-summer's day. Imagine the excitement. Off on holidays to Cork. I had mostly packed my bag the evening before because I was staying at my grandmother's that night. We stayed over there quite often. Sometime around noon, Fr Smyth landed in his blue Renault four car – that's the one with the distinctive gear shift which came out of the dashboard. He arrived and went in to talk to the adults, and I finished the packing upstairs: the toothbrush and toothpaste.

Next thing, he walks in through the bedroom door and says, 'How's it going? Everything ready?' I says, 'Yes'. Then he put his two hands to my face, either cheek, like he was cupping my wee head. He tells me to give him a hug and pulls me tight and kisses me full on the lips. All this in about two seconds. I was utterly astonished; I didn't know what to do. I got this shivery feeling all down inside, deeply uncomfortable. He didn't say anything and just walked away and down the stairs.

Jesus, what was that? Was it right? Was it wrong? I didn't know but I did know it was strange behaviour. On the other hand, Fr Smyth was a priest so it had to be all right. I just left it to the one side and continued on, got my stuff and went downstairs, said goodbye and away we went.

We travelled up to Belfast, where he collected a girl. She lived off the Falls Road in west Belfast. She was very pretty, and to this day I remember her name and her address. I've called her 'Belfast Girl'.

Fr Smyth then headed south, this time to a farmhouse in rural County Cavan. A proper farmhouse, with a big range in the kitchen. There was a girl there, who I was told was also coming with us. I'll call her 'Cavan Girl'. He walked into the place like he owned it and introduced me and Belfast Girl, explaining that we would be all going with him on the trip in the morning. I stayed there overnight and he went back to his abbey to sleep.

In the morning, he returned and this time he had a lad with him – a quiet-spoken boy who was a year or so older than me. He'll be 'Cavan Boy'. It may be that we picked Cavan Boy up after we left the farmhouse, I am not sure, but I know that we then finally headed off to Cork itself.

So there we were, the four us, in Fr Smyth's car heading south, all the way to Cork. It would cause heads to turn now, I suspect, if you saw a priest, all in black, travelling with four assorted youngsters, average age eleven. But in those times it wasn't the slightest bit remarkable.

It was a huge expedition. Between the stops and starts a six- or seven-hundred-mile round trip. There were sweets to make the journey that bit shorter and there were regular meal stops for burgers and chips and a soft drink. He treated us well – anything we wanted, we got.

I can remember us all singing and clapping along to songs, the Beatles. I can't remember who instigated this, possibly he did. We were a shy bunch and no one was likely to start the singing without his encouragement.

We drove to a monastery in Cork, in Cork city. There were a few monks about, but it didn't seem particularly big. Straight away, he celebrated mass. We all helped. I can remember the smell of polish yet, and the darkened, ancient wood, and long corridors with all the doors with round knobs. A spooky sort of place.

We had a meal, watched some television and then it was time to go to bed. I can't be certain but I think it may have been at the monastery or it may have been a bed & breakfast. I do remember the boys' bedroom had two beds, one for me and Cavan Boy, the other for Fr Smyth.

The lights were out when he called me over to his bed. He put me into the bed beside him. He pulled me close and then he put his hand down on my private parts. He took my hand and placed it on his penis.

Then he pulled my pyjamas down and he pulled his own down. And then he started rubbing and pulling at me and making me rub and pull him. I remember him going, 'Faster! Harder!' And kissing me too, pushing his lips at me.

I didn't know what the hell was going on. I just wanted this to be over and to get back into my own bed.

Then he ejaculated and that was that. I was sent back to bed. After a little while, he called the other boy over. Did the same to him. I heard everything. I couldn't watch; I kept my head well tucked down in the bed clothes. I was relieved that it wasn't me this time but I was anxious that he might call me back. My head was in a spin.

All sorts of things were happening to me for the first time and none of it felt right. It just had the whole air of being wrong. But Fr Smyth was a priest, a good man; all were agreed on that. So I thought, perhaps it's OK and I'm just being funny about it.

I did have a whispered emergency chat with Cavan Boy afterwards. Both of us agreed it was weird, but I think we also thought it must be OK because it was Fr Smyth and he was a priest and couldn't do wrong. But, in my heart of hearts, I already knew that some rule had been broken. I just wasn't sure what rule.

Did he pay a visit to the girls' room that night? I don't know.

In the morning we just got up for early mass and then had breakfast before heading to Blarney Castle. We all got a chance to kiss the Blarney Stone. I bought a stick of rock, and some wee present for Mammy and then we were off again, back home.

We were passing Dundalk and I said, 'You can drop me off.'

'No, No! We will go to Belfast first.'

So he went up to Belfast, down to Cavan and then across to Dundalk. I was the last one he dropped off, and he came into the house and had tea with my mother and father. I'm sure he was looking for thanks and praise, having taken me off for a wee break.

I just wanted to forget about it. I didn't want to think about it. I didn't want him to come back into the house again. A week or two later, he came back. I wanted to get out of the place and fled upstairs to do my homework.

Minutes passed and I thought I was safe. Then the sound of his steps, and his voice calling out, 'Sure I'll help him with his homework. No bother.'

And he abused me up in my bedroom as he had done in Cork.

* * *

Before I knew it, this became a regular occurrence. Downstairs, Mammy and Daddy were utterly oblivious to what the nice priest was doing to their wee boy above the ceiling. Their devotion to him was part of the locking device he had on the truth getting out. My parents were so in awe of him, and what he represented, that I felt I had no choice but to continue to obey Fr Smyth.

I knew that I wasn't to speak about it to others. Fr Smyth told me it was 'our secret'.

My grooming period was well and truly over. There was little pretence any more. He would find any excuse to take me out in the car with him, to serve mass at Mount Oliver or to visit some sick person. At the first opportunity, he would pull the car in off the road and start to fondle me and instruct me to fondle him.

It was almost simulated sex, with him crouched on top of me, though he never attempted to rape me. I now know that while he favoured prepubescent boys he would abuse girls of all ages, right up to their late teens. I have heard of some girls being raped by him, but I don't think his abuse was as invasive with boys.

And then he came to the school and visited. I remember a couple of times I was in class at school, and the head brother would come down and call me out of class for a special visitor.

The first time this happened there was a look from the others in the class – a look that said 'lucky you', getting out of Irish lessons, or whatever. That first time I looked back at them with the start of a grin, enjoying the moment. Inside, I was nervous, not sure who awaited me.

'It's Fr Smyth for you.'

Jaysůs! The tummy fell away from me, but there was no stopping this journey. Off with me down a corridor to a parlour, somewhere private, where I would find Fr Smyth waiting for me.

The door would close. The room was out of the way, so it was unlikely that anybody would walk past or interrupt him. There was a large oval table with dining chairs around it. Beside them were a couple of armchairs and a sofa. He'd choose the sofa and then call me close, pulling me onto his lap.

He would chat to me, for a moment, before he began abusing me. Normally, this involved wanking him. When he had his pleasure, he would dole out some sweets and away with him. It was as functional as that.

The next time around there was the same response from my classmates: 'He's away again, the lucky fecker.' But I didn't show any excitement or even fear.

I was expressionless for I had no control, good, bad or indifferent, over what was going to happen next.

I did get smarter. The abuse eased off in the home when I figured out how to outwit him. The moment I heard he was arriving, I would land down in whatever room my parents were in. If I was in my bedroom, I could see the car outside. Down the stairs I would go at ninety miles an hour.

Come hell or high water, I wouldn't leave my parents' side. That stopped it in the home, more or less, but it was impossible for me to get out of helping old people or serving mass for the nuns. So the abuse continued, in his car, with him straddling me like an animated scarecrow.

* * *

Christmas 1974, or thereabouts, The Wombles were huge all over Britain and Ireland. They were on a big tour and one of the concerts was scheduled for Dublin. Fr Smyth landed at the house one evening and suggested that he take me on a trip to see them. Not just me but my two younger sisters too, Moira and Eilish.

My parents thought it was a great idea, another act of kindness and generosity by Fr Smyth. A pantomime was on offer too. We were told he was coming to pick us up. I think it was on a Friday night. He arrived and he had two children with him in the car. These children were new to me, a brother and sister from Belfast.

The boy was good-looking and swarthy, great fun even though he was a little older than me. His sister was younger but laughed a lot too. Nice kids. They came into the house and met my parents. We all had tea and biscuits before heading off.

Children must have great capacity to fool themselves. Or maybe kids learn to compartmentalise their troubles because I don't recall being anxious heading away on this trip. It could be that because I was with my sisters and the other kids I simply didn't give any thought to the prospect of being attacked again. Or maybe that was the spell that Fr Smyth had on us all.

The run to Dublin takes less than an hour now but back then, in 1974, it was a good two hours in his wee car. I brought along my own tape of the Beatles. He was delighted with that and thought it a gift and kept it. But that wasn't the intention – the intention was to play it and bring it home.

When we got to Dublin, he took us first to a guest house. It was in Drumcondra, in one of those very large, red-bricked homes close to Croke Park on the north side of Dublin.

In we went and put our stuff away, then off to the concert. I don't know what venue it was in, but we were sitting all in a line and he was sitting right behind us. The concert was great, lots of cheering and shouting.

And then the worry started. Back to the guest house, where the alarm bells went off. It was the same scenario. He had the three girls in one room and the two boys in the same room as him. I was to share a bed with Belfast Boy. Fr Smyth had the other bed in the room.

I was no longer quite as compliant with the abuse. Maybe the fact that Belfast Boy and me got on so well emboldened me, because I suggested to him that we stay in the girls' room that night. He agreed, knowingly.

Fr Smyth was still downstairs, talking to the landlady or watching TV, when we went out along the landing and found the girls' room. I remember knocking, knocking hard on the door. They let us in, but just as quick they were telling us to go back to our own room.

We were virtually begging them to allow us to stay in their room for the night, to sleep on the floor, or whatever, but they just laughed at that and ordered us out. They thought we were only messing about. And of course we were not going to say what the real reason was that we wanted in; that was impossible. Back to our bedroom and our fate.

The bedroom was washed in darkness with sprinkles of light. It wasn't pure black. The curtains weren't pulled tight or maybe they were too thin to keep out the street lighting. So you could see shapes. In particular, I could see the skinny shadow of Belfast Boy when he did as instructed and left our bed and crossed the room. He was first for the treatment that night.

I was lying in the bed, waiting my turn, head under the blankets; I was listening in trepidation. Sounds of scratching, rubbing, the odd panicky words from Belfast Boy, everything was amplified. The heavy breathing of Fr Smyth, the noise was overwhelming. Like the rumble of a huge truck bearing down on you. My turn next.

I am thinking this is not going to happen again. I am not doing this anymore. I am like a fucking cow waiting to come into the slaughter house, in a bloody queue. No, I am not having this no more. This was somehow worse, far worse, than the assaults in the car or the bedroom. It brought home to me how he had all of us at his mercy. Any child. All children.

When he finished with Belfast Boy, he called me over and I went to him. And he did his usual thing. I was powerless. He pulled at me and this time for the first time in my life I had an orgasm. I didn't even know what it was, but there was pleasure in it. Can you imagine how mixed up I was? My first sexual moment was with a priest. What do you think that does to you? I would find that out later, deep in teenage years. I still live with it and the consequences.

That night was really the deciding moment for me. I had to stop this. I had started secondary school, was starting puberty. Sex had entered my language and, though I knew little about it, I understood it had something to do with ejaculation, and women.

There we were, me and Belfast Boy, united in terror and shame, terrified of speaking up about it. Because of the authority and the reputation of Fr Smyth there was no way we could stop this on our own. He never threatened me with violence. His power over me was such that no threat was necessary.

The following morning there was mass again in a little church or chapel nearby. There was always a mass involved somewhere. Then away to see Maureen Potter in the pantomime in the Gaiety Theatre. Incredible when you think of what had just gone on overnight.

Finally, the journey home via Belfast. We dropped off Belfast Boy and his sister. We had the regulation tea and biscuits there with their family before Fr Smyth took me and my sisters home.

The terrible fear and unease that had taken me over in the bedroom that night, while I awaited my turn with Fr Smyth, returned to me in the days and nights afterwards. I remember odd bits and pieces: the smell of the car with its strange air freshener and the addresses of the children who were with me. Other memories are completely lost in the bedlam of that time, but the details of the abuse, the groping, the shame of all of it, is clear as day.

I was getting to the point where I knew I would do something. That terrible night in Dublin had scared me. I had felt paralysed. I was imagining the possibility of Fr Smyth getting at the girls. This had been their first time away with him, and I was thinking that, in time, he would make a move on them too. I resolved that I would never let that happen.

But it did happen to me again. And again. When you read the accounts that abuse victims give of what happened to them twenty, twenty-five years ago, you might wonder why they tend not to be able to be specific about dates. I understand that. The dates blur into each other. I can't tell you how many times I was taken away in Fr Smyth's car and abused by the side of the road, or down some laneway. Nor can I tell you how often he came to my bedroom, but I can tell what happened there.

As it happens, I know that Fr Smyth assaulted me on several more occasions after The Wombles' trip. In my bedroom. And on the road too.

The fact is that I couldn't be on guard duty all the time. If I wasn't paying absolute attention, Fr Smyth would be in the house, stepping up to my bedroom with one arm outstretched to open and close the door behind him.

The last time was St Patrick's Day, 1975. There, I remembered that. St Patrick, who chased the snakes out of Ireland. And the time before that was 16 March, the previous day. My parents were out at a dance that evening when Fr Smyth landed. There was no cover for me, so I was abused yet again.

* * *

The incidents of abuse had piled up. By this time, I'd been assaulted maybe two dozen times by Fr Smyth. He'd abused me where, when and how he wanted. I was a toy thing for him to play with at his leisure, but I was getting a little wiser. I had just turned fourteen and wasn't quite as naive as I had been when he'd first preyed on me.

Chapter 4
Growing Up, Speaking Out

The time of reckoning was fast approaching. I was starting to grow into my own life, developing my own personality, as opposed to the imagined personality expected of me by my family. Like others my age I was beginning to take charge of my life, though if it was a teenage rebellion it was a very quiet one.

Looking back, there were landmark moments. I had started to go to mass on my own. At first, Mammy would ask me about the sermon, checking up on me. I always knew the answer, so this wasn't a drama. Then I started to skip mass as often as not and say nowt to my parents. Telling them would have prompted a confrontation and I was still reluctant to openly challenge my parents. Their authority was clear if unspoken.

The priests in the Holy Redeemer Parish were nice enough. The parish priest, Fr Owen Sweeney, was a gentleman. Then there was Fr Seán McCartan. He was a real friend of the family, a regular visitor. My conversations with all these priests were, I am sure, typical of other children of the time: 'Yes, Father. No, Father.' Those chats were like an extension of the Confession box, head down, sins a' swimming. Nevertheless, nice as they were, I found it difficult to trust them due to my previous experience with Fr Smyth.

Confession was proving more difficult for me at this time. I stopped going. I was innocent, so much more innocent than children today but I wasn't deaf. The school yard was where you had your sex education. If there was any sex education in the classroom, it was through the biology class.

'Penis.'

'Vagina.'

Once the science teacher uttered those words, the place would erupt, waves of nervous giggles spreading through the room.

I wasn't laughing, though. For me this was holy terror. Biology was all about man and woman. Husband and wife. The books said nothing about priests grappling with an altar boy's penis. Sitting there in De La Salle secondary school, it was clear to me that whatever Fr Smyth was doing to me it was clearly linked to sex. It was equally clear to me that it was unnatural.

Out in the school yard the distinction was even clearer. Out there, at lunchtime, the chat would be about willies and fannies, pussies and tits. There was no talk about priests coming over your hand and you taking a hankie to wipe his stuff away.

There was talk, though, of dirty old men who might attempt to have their way with you. Different lads would tell stories about one local man or another.

'You have to watch out getting a lift with yer man. He'll slap the hand on your willie before you know it.'

Others would tell tales of how they were nearly trapped by some old lad but managed to get away. They told these stories like they had taken part in some epic adventure: 'The Great Escape'. There was all sorts of advice as to what to do if some fella came onto you: 'Punch him in the balls. Kick him in the head. Get the lads down to kick the shite out of him.'

I didn't contribute much to these discussions for obvious reasons. Even listening to the conversations was difficult for me. I was that fella who had been trapped by the old boy. I was that kid who had been got at. And I hadn't done anything about it.

Around this time my school work started to suffer. I was constantly worrying about Fr Smyth and about my own reaction to him. Why hadn't I done anything?

Was it me? My fault? The other lads were talking about being so brave, but here was me terrified of even thinking about it. And doing nothing. And my sisters and God knows how many others out there were still lining up to be used by him. I was at an age that I felt I should be in charge of my life, but clearly I wasn't.

My dilemma was simple: I wanted to put a stop to it but I had no idea how. It just wasn't an option going to Mammy and Daddy. My grandparents were off-limits for the same reason. There was no other adult that I trusted to help me, no teacher, no aunt or uncle.

Then I came across the first priest that I totally trusted, Fr Oliver McShane. Fr McShane was officially based at the Dominican Priory in Dundalk (the Priory was known locally as the Friary). He was chaplain to Dundalk vocational school and also ran the St Dominic's boys' and girls' club. He was popular, in part because he was young, only a few years ordained, and in part because he appeared to take a genuine interest in us kids.

A friend of mine, Joe Ralph, had been going on about the youth club. We sat beside each other in school and he would tell me about how great it was – St Dominic's Youth Club. There was table tennis, any number of other games and a cool young priest who ran it and encouraged you to chat.

So I started going there with him. The club was in a big prefabricated hall, squeezed in beside the Friary and the adjacent church on Anne Street. It was across town from Marian Park, so I didn't know most of those there. It was a very strange feeling at first. There were lots of new faces from the area around Oriel Park football ground, home to Dundalk Town FC. And there was this young priest, Fr Oliver McShane, who kept on saying, in a soft northern accent, at the start of each session: 'If anyone has got any problems, come and chat to me. No matter how big or how small it is.'

And I said to myself, this is my opportunity now. That first meeting decided me but I still wasn't ready to talk about it. I was just too nervous, too scared of his reaction. So I got cold feet and I didn't speak up, but I went home and I promised myself I would speak to him about my problem the next week.

Fr McShane was different from all the other priests I had known. He was much younger for a start. He couldn't have been much older than thirty and he had an air of craic about him. There was nothing remote about him the way there was with all the priests I had known (Fr Smyth being the exception). Tall and wide, with dark curly hair, he looked like a country guard, though you couldn't take that image too far because he wore an all-white cassock.

I went to the club the following week, played the games, and again he asked if anyone had any problems, encouraging us to speak up. My resolve deserted me again and I kept quiet.

It was Fr Smyth himself who, in a way, persuaded me to act. He came around and abused me again, one day after another, finishing up on that St Patrick's Day. I think I prayed to St Patrick, even as it was happening to me, to have the strength to finally stop this.

I had enough wit to understand that Fr Smyth must have been doing the same to many more children. I already knew what he'd done to Cavan Boy and Belfast Boy. What might happen if he got to my wee sisters, Moira and Eilish? That thought decided me.

So the next week, the third time I was there, Fr McShane repeats the invitation for anyone with a problem to chat with him. I thought, I am certain I have a problem but I don't know how serious it is. Could I be wasting this man's time? Should I trust him at all? But I wanted it to stop; I wanted an end put to it. I didn't want my sisters getting caught up in it.

It was all done discreetly. I went up to him and told him, 'Yes, I have a problem, or at least I think it's a problem.'

He says, 'That's grand. Why don't you hang around afterwards and we can have a private chat?'

My recollection of it is, we were sitting in the corner and I told him I think I have got a problem, with a priest. I said it doesn't feel right and I don't know whether it is right or it is wrong. I said I am not even sure if it is a problem. Though I did know.

So then I told him what Fr Smyth was doing, abusing me, taking me away on trips – all of that. And then I asked him again, did he think that was a problem? Did he think it was all right?

His look had long told me that it wasn't all right. He was all serious and concerned, a sense of shock about him. And then he said, 'No, Brendan, it's not all right.'

He asked me did my parents know. And of course I told him that they knew nothing. He said, 'Well, we are first going to have to tell them.'

* * *

I still had not registered the seriousness of the whole thing. I just knew what was happening to me seemed wrong, was wrong; by now I was sure it was very wrong, but I didn't understand the bigger implications.

Fr McShane took me to his car and drove down the road to my home. No messing around. Into the car and away. I realised that there was a sense of urgency associated with all of this. One minute I had held a secret that I felt bad about, the next we were about to tell the world. Or so it seemed. I was terrified about what my parents might think. Fr Smyth was their good friend, which is why of course I never said a word to them about him.

That journey took no more than five minutes, but it was an eternity for me. Would my parents believe me? I remembered how my father had taken so long to be convinced that I hadn't stolen money before. Would I get punished for this? Was this all my own fault? Most bizarrely of all, I was wondering if I had caused Fr Smyth to sin.

When we reached Marian Park, I went in first and found my mammy and daddy in the back room talking with a friend. A neighbour, I think. I went up to Daddy and whispered that there was a priest who wanted to speak to him, a Fr McShane. Daddy didn't have a clue what was going on because, though he probably knew half the priests in County Louth, he had never heard of Fr McShane.

My daddy left Mammy and her friend in the back and we all went into the front room. Fr McShane introduced himself and explained that he was there on difficult business. He said, 'You have a good son who is a brave boy. I know that you know Fr Smyth. Well, he has been abusing your son ...'

Daddy just fell back on his chair. He slumped over as if someone had hit him in the stomach. He looked ill. I know that it really hurt him. Then Fr McShane told him some of the details. I said nothing, just cried. It was like an out-of-body experience. Listening to what had happened to me replayed in front of my daddy, I was beginning to see clearly that what had happened was not just wrong but it was terribly wrong.

At one stage, my father left the room. I thought he was going to say something to my mother, but her friend was still there, so that didn't happen. Instead, he went out into the back garden and vomited. My father was getting sick in the garden because of what he had been told. I was only fourteen, but I knew he had just had the biggest shock of his life. He was devastated.

Before he left, Fr McShane told my father that the matter would have to be investigated, and he made clear that he would be reporting what he had learned to the Church authorities, immediately. I am not sure if that offered any consolation to my father. He was just bewildered by what he had heard, bewildered and upset. I don't know if he was angry. He was definitely in shock.

He never said a word to me about it when Fr McShane had gone. He just asked me if I was all right, and I said I was. Later, when the friend left, he finally told my mother. She just broke down in tears. I heard her sobbing all night.

I can well imagine why now, but then I was still unclear about the huge significance of it all. Now I understand that the nice safe world my parents had tried to construct for their children had just been smashed into pieces; it lay in smithereens about them.

Here was this man that they had been taking into their home as a dear and valued friend for more than two years and look what he had done to them. Look what he had done to their child.

They were not capable of dealing with it in a confrontational way, or maybe in any way at all. What Fr Smyth had done to me was just so far outside their sum of knowledge and experience that they couldn't possibly make sense of it. Maybe few parents could. Today would be radically different. Back then, after the first days of madness, the matter was not up for discussion.

Much later, years later, I was told about the panic that had engulfed the household that week. My father never spoke to me directly about what had happened, not to this day. It's not that he wasn't supportive, because he was, but I don't think he ever wanted to hear what happened again. That one time was enough. My mother was the same, completely supportive but not keen to speak about it.

* * *

I know it never occurred to them, in 1975, to report what had happened to the gardaí. Fr McShane didn't go to the gardaí either, but he had told my parents. The very first thing he had done was to make sure my parents knew. And then he set about alerting the Church authorities to what Fr Smyth was doing, just as he had told my parents he would.

He went back to his own place and looked up the *Catholic Directory*, which contains all the names and addresses of priests and the religious in Ireland. He found the details of the Norbertine Order at Kilnacrott easily enough but then came upon a problem.

The directory listed two Smyths at the Abbey. Or rather one Smith and one Smyth. All that he could remember from his conversation with me was that it was a Fr Smyth from Kilnacrott. To add to the confusion, the Smith (with an 'i') at the abbey was the abbot, Kevin Smith. Fr McShane realised he couldn't differentiate between the two. But there was another avenue of recourse open to him.

Fr Brendan Smyth was under the direct control of his abbot, Kevin Smith. Ultimate control of the Norbertine Order lay with the head of the order, based in Rome. I have talked to many lawyers over the years and read many legal opinions on where responsibility lay. One of these, canon law expert, Fr Tom Doyle, says that whenever Fr Smyth was in a diocese he was also under the control of the local bishop. The Abbey of the Holy Trinity at Kilnacrott was situated in the diocese of Kilmore, then under the control of Bishop Francis McKiernan. Therefore Bishop McKiernan could also exercise authority over Fr Smyth.

Fr McShane decided to bypass the abbey and pursue this avenue instead. He arranged to drive to Cavan to meet Bishop McKiernan. At the meeting he outlined what he knew.

According to Fr McShane, Bishop McKiernan informed him that this was not the first time that Fr Brendan Smyth's inappropriate activities with boys had been brought to his attention. He said the Norbertine Order, to which Fr Smyth belonged, had not taken the proper action. Bishop McKiernan went on to say that it was time the matter was dealt with properly and explained that he intended to set up an Ecclesiastical Court.

A few days after his meeting with Bishop McKiernan, Fr McShane called to our home and invited me and my father to a meeting in the Dominican Priory in Anne Street. We were left in no doubt about the gravity of this meeting, but we had no idea what it would entail.

*　*　*

There were two hugely important developments that week. The first was that I had managed to get the courage to speak up. The second was that I had been believed. One thing holding me back was the fear that I would be accused of making it up. I needn't have been so scared.

I sometimes wonder what I would have done if Fr McShane hadn't been there at the time. Would I ever have disclosed to anybody? Most times I persuade myself that whether I had spoken to him or not I would have brought an end to Fr Brendan's assaults on me sooner rather than later.

Then I wonder how I would have told my parents on my own what Fr Smyth had been doing to me.

Maybe I would have done what the lads suggested – kicked Fr Smyth in the balls. Or maybe I would have said nothing and left my sisters as prey for him.

All this is why I give thanks to Oliver McShane. He left the priesthood a few years later, married, had kids of his own and settled in London. I joined in his 70th birthday celebrations with him recently. Thank God for one good man who used to be a priest.

Chapter 5
The Secret Church Inquiry

I wouldn't have described myself as the outgoing type; I was shy, but only to a point. I look back and I don't see my childhood as totally blighted by what Fr Smyth did to me. I realise that even then I had managed to compartmentalise it. I had it in a wee box, which I carried about with me, and whenever thoughts about the abuse came to me I would lift that box up and throw it away.

I don't know if that makes sense, but it was just my way of dealing with it. The most important point was that I felt that I had assumed control of the situation. Right enough, I had been taken advantage of by a manipulating pervert, but I had managed to stop it. This meant an awful lot to me.

It was about the preservation of my very dignity. It was about me having taken responsibility for what was being done to me and then dealing with it. Or, at least, making sure it was dealt with. This was vital. I know it was the reason I managed to keep my head together through my teenage years.

I can still feel, almost in a real physical way, that resurgence in confidence which began after I spoke about the abuse to Fr McShane. Then came the meeting.

* * *

Six days had passed since my disclosure to Fr McShane and we were getting ready to set off to the meeting at the Friary. This all happened very quickly, and the very speed of it made me think that they were taking me very seriously.

Holy Saturday, 29 March 1975. It was very cold. Freezing. And getting dark. Daddy called to me and told me to wrap up – we're going around to this meeting. My mother was fussing around me: best Sunday outfit, getting a wee woolly hat for me, a scarf, warm pullover and coat.

The Friary was on Anne Street, about a mile and a half away, maybe more. We could have taken a taxi but that would have been a real luxury. So the bike it was.

Daddy's bike was one of those old-fashioned, big, black Raleighs, with a dynamo powering the front and back lights. He wasn't the type to go out without a light on the bike.

I climbed up beside him and made myself comfortable on the crossbar of the bike. I took my grip at the centre of the handlebars and tucked in under his arms. Safe.

My friends were just going in for the evening as we cycled past. There wasn't much chatter from Daddy as we headed through Marian Park into Cox's Demesne and up through Ard Easmuinn to Mount Avenue. The odd word of encouragement for me perhaps, that would have been like him.

Insulated as I was, I can still remember feeling the cold as we crossed one housing estate into another. Eventually we reached the Carrickmacross Road where the Harp brewery is. From here it was a straight spin to our destination, with just one slight incline over the railway bridge to overcome. As Daddy strained over the last stretch, I was becoming very nervous. I had no idea what was ahead of me. What was I expected to do or to say?

We had reached our destination on Anne Street. Immediately on our left was the Friary, an austere, redbrick building, with St Malachy's Church attached to the side. I slid off the crossbar and, after Daddy had chained the bike to the railings, we knocked on the door. A big thick wooden door with a tapered top – you see them in every other religious building.

I am not sure who answered, but we were ushered inside. I can remember going into this room. My father was told he had to stay outside. He was left outside in an office, where he sat alone for the next hour.

I have never had a proper chat with him about why he agreed to allow me to be quizzed about Fr Smyth alone, but he has said that he just didn't think it through. I'm sure he thought he was doing the right thing, trusting the Church to sort out Fr Smyth.

It says much about the authority the Church had that someone like him, who doted on me, would agree to sit outside while I was being questioned. He was a very good father; he took real care with me and my sisters. Yet, he was absent for one of the most stressful moments in my life.

Picture me. Shirt and tie. Pullover and creased trousers. Hair combed straight. About five foot three. Baby faced. Two months past my fourteenth birthday. Hardly even an adolescent. A child.

Inside that room with me were three priests: Fr McShane sitting beside me, there was another sitting in a chair, and one sitting on a stool on the other side. I knew one of the two other priests – Fr Francis Donnelly – because he was local. I didn't know the third priest, who was on the left-hand side, but he was to become Cardinal Seán Brady, Primate of All Ireland. Then he was plain Fr John B. Brady.

Everything that happened that evening, after the door of the meeting room closed, was pretty much lost to my memory for decades, except how I felt. My emotions. And the final words that were spoken in conversation with my daddy afterwards. I never forgot those.

I do remember being frightened. I was told that Fr McShane was there as my witness, but that didn't mean anything to me. The only thing I was sure of, sitting there alone, was that I was going to be asked about what Fr Smyth did to me.

They wanted to know if I was telling the truth or if I was a liar. As a fourteen-year-old, it felt like an inquisition. It was in fact a canonical inquiry, or an ecclesiastical court, though that wasn't clear to me at all then.

In my mind's eye they were old men in black. And if they made any effort to be non-threatening, they failed. Fr Donnelly asked most of the questions. Fr Brady took notes but I have a memory of him asking the odd question too.

The Church's own transcripts of the proceedings show the session opened with a series of basic questions. Name? Address? Date of Birth?

Then they extended into my family tree. Who was my father? Who was my mother?

If this was meant to put me at ease, it failed. They were establishing my character. Was I from a 'good' Catholic family?

Eventually the questions got down to Fr Smyth. I told them everything that I felt able to speak to them about. I am sure I held some back too. I can remember telling them that Fr Smyth asked me to 'wank' him, and Fr Donnelly asked – I will never forget this – 'What's wankle?'

That sticks in my head all the time: 'What's wankle?' That's the only thing I can remember of the questions that were asked in there.

The documentation makes clear that they were left in no doubt about what had happened. What Fr Smyth had done to me and where he had done it. I also told them about all the others on the trips; I told them about every child that was with me on the trips. Looking at the transcripts today, I can see that all those names were faithfully recorded by Fr John Brady, and the addresses too. I was even able to supply the postal code for Belfast Boy. And I explained that just as I had been abused, so too had he and Cavan Boy.

I take great satisfaction now that I had been able to provide this detail. It was all there for them, all the facts, and the names and addresses of the five kids who were being abused or who were at risk of abuse.

There was another aspect to the inquiry that leaves me full of unease, not just unease but anger and sorrow too. Even if you allow that the churchmen were obliged to ask about what Fr Smyth had done to me, some of the questions that were asked were just so totally and completely inappropriate. They are so off the wall, so open to interpretation.

Q: Would you know the meaning of the word erection?
A: No.

Q: Would you notice your penis becoming stiff?
A: Yes. Sometimes.

Q: You never got to like it?
A: No.

Q: Would you have done these things in the first place with another boy or grown-up man?
A: No.

Q: If not, why not?

A: I did not like doing this.

Q: Why did you do it with Fr Smith [sic]?

A: Because he was a priest, probably, and I did not like to refuse him.

Q: Had you any worry that it was wrong?

A: I thought it was all right when it was with a priest.

Q: You did not go to Confession for some time after that. Why?

A: It would have been embarrassing and if I had not told it, I would have thought that I made a bad Confession. I kind of wasn't sure if it was wrong.

I was no fool. Maybe naive. Maybe innocent. But I knew that the quizzing about Confession was all about me and my fault. Then I was just terrified and scared. Today I am angry, furious. Even as I am recounting this, I want to smash my fist against the bloody wall beside me.

It got worse. The very last questions come back to this theme.

Q: Did this happen between you and any other person –
   another boy and yourself for instance?
A: No. Just between me and Fr Smith [sic].

Q: Has this led to any actions with yourself?
A: Yes.

Q: Would seed come from your body as a result?
A: Yes.

So now they had established that I masturbated, alone.
Again, I felt it put blame back on me: the blame and
the shame. Because if I was masturbating, well, that
was because I enjoyed it. And if I enjoyed that, well,
then I must have enjoyed being assaulted by Fr Smyth.
Follow the logic.

*   *   *

_All signed a handwritten transcript of the original questions,
as this copy shows, signed by Fr Francis Donnelly, Brendan
Boland, Fr John B. Brady and Fr Oliver McShane._

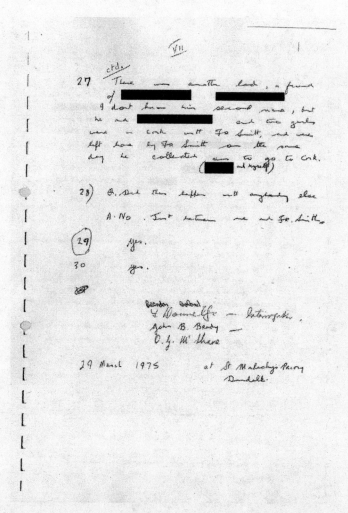

Page 7 of Fr John B. Brady's handwritten
transcription of answers from the Inquiry.

Replies of Brendan Boland

5

A. Not until I talked to Fr. McShane.

after

Q. 2I Did you tell anyone else? If so, what is his/her address?

A. No I never told anybody, only the young chap, ███████████.

Q.2B Did the other person or any other person to your knowledge do the same things with Fr. Smith ? Did they ever say they did ?

A. █████████████████████████████

Q. Low did you know ?

A. He took ███████████ and myself to the Wombles in Dublin. He did the same thing with ████████ in the bed that night and with me.

Q. Now did you know ?

A. I was awake , all in the one room.

Q. Can you remember the place ?

A. No.

Q.22 b) Did these worrying things happen in any other place besides your home and boarding houses ?

A. Yes , in the car. He would say he was going to the shop. He would pull up and do it in the car.

Q. 23 Can you give us any exact time and place at which any of these worrying things happened? In your home ? When your parents were out? When they were in ?

A. The last time was Stt Patrick's Day in the house.Before this it happened when my father and mother were at the S. and S. dance on March 16, I think.

Q. 24. Did you ever go on holidays with Fr. Smith. In the company of other boys and girls ? Was there a group of you ? Can you give us the names of those who went with you ?

A. (already answered)

Q 25 Have you planned to meet Fr. Smith again ? If so, when ?

A. Yes.

Q. When ? A Next Thursday he is supposed to be taking us for a week-end to Dublin.

Q. 26 When did you talk to Fr. McShane first ?

g̶B̶B̶.

86

Replies of Brendan Boland

6

A. On Palm Sunday, (i.e. 23 March 1975)

Q. 27 Is there anything else you would like to tell us ?

A. No . I dont think so. There was another lad, a friend of ███████
████████████████. I dont know his second name, but he and
████████████████ were in Cork with Fr. Smith, and were
left home by Fr. Smith on the same day he collected us to go to
Cork. (i.e. ████████ and myself)

~~xxx2xxx2idxxxxxxxxxppxxxxxxxxxxxybxdyxxxxxxx~~ yes

~~xxxxxyxxxxxxxxxxxxx~~ yes.

Q. 28. Did this happen between you and any other person - another

boy and yourself for instance ?

A. No. Just between me and Fr. Smith.

Q. 29 Has this led to any actions with yourself ?

A. Yes.

Q 30 Would seed come from your body as a result ?

A. Yes.

Questions put by me: Signed P. Donnelly.

Brendan Boland. Witness

John B. Brady. Notary

O. G. McShane. Witness.

29 March 1975 at St. Malachy's Priory, Dundalk.

The replies were then confirmed by oath as follows:

I Brendan Boland , hereby swear that I have told the truth the
whole truth and nothing but the truth and that I will talk to no one
about this interview except authorized priests.

Signed Brendan Boland.

John B. Brady.

29.3. 1975.

bon cordat cum orig.
John B. Brady

*The transcript of the actual proceedings was written up by
Fr John B. Brady (Cardinal Brady). Names of other children
have been redacted. Seen in black and white the nature
of some of the questions is very unsettling.*

See why I am also so sad? My father, my loving, decent, caring father, sat outside that room, quiet and as obliging as a pet dog, while the Church took charge of his little boy and did its level best to make sure this little child understood exactly how complicit he was in all of this.

The main transcript, typed up and signed as a true copy of proceedings by Fr John B. Brady concludes with details as to who was present and their role. It also spells out an oath that I signed.

The document states that Fr Donnelly put the questions, that Fr Brady was a notary, and that Fr McShane was a witness. I was also a witness according to this paperwork.

The oath must have been the last element of the inquiry. I remember putting my hand on a bible, swearing an oath and then putting down my signature. The oath itself was handwritten and then countersigned beneath. It reads:

I Brendan Boland, hereby swear that I have told the truth, the whole truth and nothing but the truth and that I will talk to no one about this interview except authorized [sic] priests.

I Brendan Boland, hereby
swear that I have told
the truth the whole truth
and nothing but the
truth and that I will
talk to no one about
this interview ~~to to~~
~~to~~ except authorized
Priests.

brendan boland.

John B. Brady
29. 3. 1975.

Copy of my written oath, countersigned by
Fr John B. Brady (Cardinal Brady).

There are two signatures underneath this. The first is my own. A tiny, joined-up nervous squiggle – Brendan Boland. The second signature, delivered with a confident flourish, is that of John B. Brady – later Cardinal Seán Brady.

I had forgotten about the oath until my lawyers later fell upon it. I blanked it, just like I had blanked so much of the actual proceedings. But the oath did its job. I had buried the whole process in a conscious act of forgetting because I had made an oath of silence. That's the only explanation I have for not remembering. This fourteen-year-old boy simply understood he was to say nothing. To anybody.

When we were finished my father was called in, or we went out to join him. He was animated, worried. Two things concerned him mostly:

His first question: 'Would Fr Smyth pose a threat to Brendan again?'

He was given assurances that this was not a possibility. Fr Smyth would be dealt with. He would not be a threat to children again.

The second question: 'Would Fr Smyth's actions have a lasting impact on Brendan?'

My father isn't sure whether it was Fr Donnelly or Cardinal Brady, but one of them turned to him and said. 'Sorry, Mr Boland, but you will have our prayers.'

My father's main concern was that I would be all right, that I would turn out OK. That this hadn't changed me. And they turned to him and said they would pray for him and pray for me. He's said since that, at that point, he wasn't interested in their prayers; he just wanted to know what impact the abuse would have on me.

I never told Daddy about what had happened inside that room, about the questions that had been asked. The questions that now appear to me to have been insinuating that I was instigating the assaults. Nor did I tell him about the oath. Of course not, wasn't I sworn to secrecy?

He didn't find out until very recently and I know it nearly crushed him. It sickened him. Here he was, my super daddy, who tried so hard to mind and protect us all, and not only had I been abused in the very sanctuary of our home, but I had been put through this secret process too.

None of this was his fault, but I know he blames himself for not protecting me. My mammy likewise. He and Mammy are not the first parents to blame themselves, but they didn't understand exactly how clever and devious abusers like Fr Smyth were. As for the role of the Church, well, it was all-powerful and as far as true believers were concerned it could do no wrong. Anyone who disputes this wasn't living in Ireland in those times.

Fr McShane, my protector, was another one duped. Like my father he trusted the Church authorities to deal with this. He was as brainwashed as my parents. In his defence, he had acted with urgency and went out and rang the alarm bells. Immediately.

He must have felt certain that Fr Smyth's days as an abuser were over.

I did. So did my father. It had been an ordeal, but I was safe. So too were my sisters. And Cavan Girl and Belfast Girl and Cavan Boy and Belfast Boy. And their friends, at least one of whom I had also mentioned in the inquiry.

At the time, I was just glad it was over. It had been very scary. It was like going to Confession but with three inquisitors, not the one. One big confessional. There were no 'Hail Marys' to say afterwards, though, and I don't remember any signs of anger towards me. The atmosphere was controlled.

Maybe the best comparison is a courtroom. When I read reports of rape victims being taken over their evidence, I think of that evening. I know how they feel, with notional complicity always lurking, unsaid, in the background, no matter the circumstances of the case.

* * *

Back on the bike and home. The first building we passed on the journey was Dundalk Garda Station. We couldn't miss it. It stands on the opposite corner to the Friary. I often wonder would things have turned out differently if that had been our destination that evening. What would have happened if, instead of trusting in the Church, we had gone directly to the proper authorities and demanded that they deal with this abusing priest?

The answer is maybe not that much. Inquiries of recent years have revealed that, on occasion, gardaí ignored the reports that did come to them, or mishandled them, or even actively helped cover up. I am not aware of one case from that era that ended up in the courts, though we now know that clerical abuse went back decades. It's as if the whole society was blinded by the power of the Church.

In reality, I think we all thought the Church was above the gardaí. It had been reported to the Church, so let them deal with it. But there was more to it than that. If a young girl had been attacked and raped by an ordinary citizen, the police would have been called. But if the rapist had been a priest? Well ...

Chapter 6
Not Alone

There was one problem. I was supposed to go away on another trip with Smyth, to Dublin with Belfast Boy and his sister. My sisters were to come too. My parents must have been in a right fix about it. How could they stop it? They never discussed it in front of me, but I can well imagine the drama.

No matter what they knew, they would have been very uncomfortable with a full-blown confrontation with the man they had trusted so willingly with their son, and their daughters too. The very idea of him arriving at the door, all smiles, all sweets, must have been terrifying for them. They were quiet people, remember, who would struggle to get angry, and would have had real difficulty in facing him down.

My parents knew that Smyth had arranged to visit on the Thursday, five days after the inquiry. Daddy was due to start work at ten, which would have meant that my mother would have been alone in the house if Fr Smyth arrived before two o'clock when Daddy returned. My mother was terrified that he was going to come. So first thing the next morning, my father went to the local parochial house to see a priest there, Fr Seán McCartan.

This priest was a real friend of the family. When my father knocked at the door, the housekeeper answered and said Fr McCartan was at his breakfast – could it wait? My father said, 'No. Tell him Frank Boland is here to see him.'

Fr McCartan left his breakfast and called my father inside. He had no idea what the matter was, but he would have surmised it had to be an emergency – of a private nature.

My father told me later that Fr McCartan actually swore when he heard the story. Daddy asked him if he would do guard duty with my mother in case Fr Smyth landed. Fr McCartan said, 'I won't let him in the feckin' door.'

The day came. The family was all on tenterhooks, wondering if the message had got through. We were off school for Easter and hanging around the house. The appointed time came and went, and no sign of Smyth. I was delighted. My parents had been wound up, but as the hours passed they relaxed too. Smyth never arrived. I now know, from a statement Fr McCartan made to the gardaí, that he sent a telegram to the abbey in Kilnacrott, advising Fr Smyth not to visit, saying that Brendan Boland wouldn't be going out with him. He also stated that he spoke to his own superiors locally, who in turn made contact with either the diocese of Kilmore or the Norbertine Order at Kilnacrott.

* * *

I felt sure that the cancelled trip marked the last of my dealings with Fr Smyth. But I was wrong. Three days later he reappeared.

It was the following Saturday and I was at work, a part-time job I had at a butcher's shop in Marian Park. I remember looking out the window and seeing a familiar car. So I looked again, and it was the flipping blue Renault four with Smyth at the wheel. He pulled the car up outside the shop. He opened the window and waved his finger, pointed his finger at me.

I knew what he was saying, 'I know that you have squealed on me.' Then he drove off.

I was really scared after that. My journey home that night was all in terror. It was cold, with a thick smoky fog down low on the ground. Every step I took, I was sure that he would be parked up around the next corner. I ran from corner to corner, checking out the little bit of ground I could see, like a frightened wild animal, before I scurried along the next stretch. I was all nerves, shaking and near crying, until I reached home.

I have thought about that scene many times since. He had spent more than two years trying to convince me that he was a kindly uncle type. Those boxes of sweets. The trips. I suppose there was no need to pretend any more. I had denied him his sweeties, his little pleasures, so I had to be told off.

The fear, though, was very real. I can still see myself hunched and alone in the fog. And, yet, I wonder what I was worried about, because all the time I knew him I never saw him angry. He never raised his hand and beat one of us. My own conclusion is that I was afraid of what he represented; I was afraid of his authority through God. I was afraid of God.

I never said a word to Mammy or Daddy, not a word about it. I was afraid that it would come back to me, that I might be blamed. You see, it was never said outright, but I felt that in the middle of this trouble with Smyth there was shame, or wrong, and that I was in some way responsible. This was never clearly said, but because of the questioning I had come through and because of the secrecy that was imposed on me I figured it out anyway. Not that I blame my parents for that, it's just the way it was.

As far as communications between me and my parents were concerned the matter was finished as a point of conversation the week of the inquiry. It was never spoken of again until Smyth hit the headlines in 1994. It was behind us and was going to stay there, out of sight and, we all hoped, out of mind too.

* * *

Elsewhere Fr John B. Brady was staying busy. He has not revealed if he actually spoke to his superior, Bishop McKiernan, about what had transpired at the inquiry with me, but he has explained generally what he did next. Other details emerged in various investigations and through records which were produced in my own legal proceedings.

Fr Brady made contact with Cavan Boy, one of the lads who I had said had also been abused. I had given his name and address. Six days after my inquiry Fr Brady met with Cavan Boy in the home of a parish priest, local to where the boy lived. To be fair to him, Fr Brady was acting with speed. That can't be denied.

Cavan Boy was a little older than me but not much wiser. He was told to attend the parochial house for a chat about Fr Smyth.

This time Fr Brady asked the questions; he also took down the answers. The parish priest was present but doesn't appear to have had any role to play other than attempting to put the boy at his ease. As the Church would later confirm in a press statement, Fr Brady conducted this part of the inquiry.

The questions weren't as invasive as the ones I faced. I assume this is because, as he himself has since explained, Fr Brady was just looking for verification of my account.

Cavan Boy was asked about 'worrying things' that had reportedly happened with Fr Smyth. He told how he had been on trips to the cinema with Smyth, accompanied by other boys around the same age. The trips were regular occurrences, about once a month, he explained.

Then it was down to the detail. Cavan Boy outlined how he was abused.

Smyth would often drop him last and then take the opportunity to abuse him. Fr Brady was told how Fr Smyth would make the boy touch his penis, then he would grope the boy. As with me, Cavan Boy was asked if he liked it, and, as with me, Cavan Boy answered 'No'.

He confirmed that he had been on holiday with me and others. And he told how the two of us had discussed the abuse one time.

That was my account verified. But there was more.

Cavan Boy was asked who else had been with him, what other children were on the trips. And he reeled off two of the names and, again, the addresses that I had given – Cavan Girl, for example. Then he told of other children, boys, who I had never met but who Fr Smyth took with him on his trips to the cinema. There were three of them, all local to Cavan Boy.

Cavan Boy was also asked if these things had any influence on his life. He said, 'Not much.' I think that is an interesting answer, because to me it suggests the abuse had *some* impact on him. There is no evidence that this reply was followed up. Mind you, I wasn't asked the question at all.

This phase of the canonical inquiry ended with Cavan Boy being made to swear an oath. The wording differed slightly to mine, not that I think it makes any difference.

His reads:

I, XXX XXX, hereby swear that I have told the truth, the whole truth, and nothing but the truth and that I will not discuss this interview with anybody except priests who have permission to discuss it. So help me God and those holy Gospels which I touch.

The oath is signed by Cavan Boy, in plain, big print, and then countersigned by Fr John B. Brady. In the transcript Fr Brady's role is entitled: 'Interrogator'.

I did not know any of this back then, nor did I know about the very particular circumstances of this second inquiry.

I had been interviewed alone, without my father, who'd been left outside. That was wrong, but at least my parents had an inkling of what was going on. They weren't told about the oath of secrecy nor about the information I had given the Church. However, they had been told that I had been abused and thus were able to protect me from further assaults. They knew enough to cancel that trip away with Smyth.

Cavan Boy's parents were told nothing, not a word. His parents were totally unaware of the Church investigation. His father wasn't in any ante-room; he was in complete ignorance. The Church also failed to tell the parents that their son had been abused by Fr Smyth. The boy said nothing because as far as he was concerned he'd made an oath and he kept his oath.

Up until this point Fr Brady had been efficiency itself. Examining his notes of proceedings, it is clear that he took great care to record the names and the addresses of the children that Cavan Boy and I had revealed. He had made sure to verify my account.

One week later, Fr Brady submitted two reports to his superior, Bishop McKiernan. Bishop McKiernan then reported the findings to Abbot Smith at Kilna-crott and between them they came up with a way to punish Fr Brendan Smyth. Fr Smyth was barred from his priestly duties, in the Abbey and in the diocese of Kilmore, for an unspecified period. Bishop McKiernan also advised psychiatric intervention.

Fr Tom Doyle, the canon law expert, says the Church had clearly established that Fr Smyth was abusing children. He says that this should then have been brought to a full ecclesiastical court hearing. The outcome of this court should, if the facts were proven, have been the defrocking of Smyth. He would have lost the uniform which so helped his predatory behaviour. And dozens of other children might have been spared child sexual abuse.

I've often heard it said that the Church had no notion that clerics were abusing children, but Fr Doyle, who first started investigating clerical abuse in the 1980s in America, says that's not true. He say that the Church knew enough about such abuse to legislate for it. He points out that child abuse was listed as a crime in the first promulgation of the Code of Canon Law (1917) and repeated in the present, revised edition in Canon 1395 (2):

'A cleric who in another way has committed an offense against the sixth commandment of the Decalogue, if the delict was committed by force or threats or publicly or with a minor below the age of sixteen years, is to be punished with just penalties, not excluding dismissal from the clerical state if the case so warrants'.

Chapter 7
First Love

It seems extraordinary now, but it was as if Smyth had gone from the face of the earth. His name was never mentioned. He'd vanished. I suppose my parents hoped memories of him would disappear too. He stayed in my head because of the whole sex thing, but he certainly wasn't there every waking moment, or anything like that.

As a child I had taken my faith probably a wee bit more seriously than others my age. That faith had been impacted by all that had happened. I never did return to Confession, unless I was policed into it at school. And mass, well, that had become an exercise in escapology. When I realised that I could decide if I went or not, I chose not to go. Instead of going into the chapel, I would head off for a walk, sometimes meeting up with like-minded mates. The trick was to know who had said the mass and the gist of the sermon of the day. A quick chat with another friend who had attended sorted that.

This cover-up of mine lasted only so long. I wasn't very good at lying, so it ended in the confrontation that I'd been dreading. I remember there was a shouting match. I was told that I was committing a sin by not going to mass. Eventually Daddy relented. He wasn't happy, but he wasn't going to force me to go once he saw I had my mind made up.

* * *

In the years immediately following the canonical inquiry what Daddy did was pretty amazing. He devoted all his spare time to entertaining the four of us. I don't think he let us out of his sight. At the time I half resented it, but he's revealed since that it was about making sure we were safe at all times.

Music was how he did this. My own interest had matured from the accordion to the guitar. My father had this senior citizens' club and I used to go round. There was a nun there, Sister de Paris, and she used to play the guitar, so my father asked her would she give the kids in the area guitar lessons. She said she would.

The committee got together and they bought a load of guitars and anybody that wanted to go to guitar lessons could attend. I remember starting off and the first song I ever learned was 'Kumbaya, My Lord'. It was easy; it was in the key of D, only three chords in it.

My sister, Anne, would sing at the club accompanied by her friend Patricia Duffy on piano. They were happy for me to strum along on guitar. Patricia would shout out the chords to me, which is how I learned to play. Week in, week out, I would play, and I would spend hours at home practising.

Daddy also organised talent shows for the local children. And then took them on the road. Mad-cap stuff when you think about it. Off we would traipse in a hired minibus to one border village or another and put on a show. Some comedy. Some songs. Some dancing.

He was always with us. Everywhere we went. From Cullaville to Crossmaglen and different parts around Dundalk itself. The shows always started off with a big dancing routine, everyone in costume. Massive fun.

Anne, Patricia and myself wanted to have a proper band: Anne singing, an amazing voice she has, and Patricia on the piano. We got a drummer, Mark Kelly, and borrowed the keys of the hall, so we could go round and practice.

We called ourselves Low Volume. Less said about the name the better but it sort of made sense. We had one speaker between us. Off we went to seek our fame and fortune in the bars and pubs about Dundalk and out the road as far as Castlebellingham. Weddings too. A fiver a night, we started at; that grew to £20.

After a year or so, Mark left. We then found a new drummer, Terry Savage, and we also added a bass player, Paddy McEneaney, and we changed our name. Low Volume became Tanya. My father had a big influence on the name. He pushed for it because we had a cat of the same name, and because he also liked Tanya Tucker, the singer. He was our number one groupie, following us from gig to gig, keeping an eye out.

Anne and myself were to be in one final band, Santa Fe (we never were great with names). We were joined by Eugene Fee, Dessie Gernon and Ollie Reynolds; we played together for a while until we went our separate ways.

School ended with the intermediate exams. The 'Inter' we called it, and I did all right in it. My studies never really picked up after the Smyth drama, but I wasn't too concerned. I was never going to go on to college. Back then, many, maybe most, of the lads would have left school at this stage, off to earn a wage. Some into the factories, others into apprenticeships.

Still, after I did badly in my pre-inter exams, I was worried that I wouldn't do well enough to get any work offers afterwards.

Anne's boyfriend, Jimmy Flynn, was doing an evening course at college in Dundalk. He advised me to go with him and study in the library while he attended his course. I went along with him for a couple of months leading up to my exams. This proved to be invaluable as I achieved the results needed to get an apprenticeship as an electrician. Thank you, Jimmy.

I headed off to Evan Henry's, an electrical contractor in the town. My grandfather worked in there as a storeman. The boss, Evan Henry, was friendly with my grandfather. He was best man at my uncle's wedding, so it really wasn't too difficult to get a job with him.

I landed on my feet there, no mistake. My grandfather, God rest him, did me a big favour. This was the time of five-year apprenticeships; there were no shortcuts like there are now. I even ended up in college, doing three-month block release placements down in Carlow.

The money the first year wasn't great, but it improved. And I got driving too. My father bought his first car but actually shared it between me and Anne, a Fiat 124.

He was something else on the road, one of those thousands of folk who were unleashed on the Irish road because the government in its wisdom, in 1979, decided the best way to clear the log jam of applications was to allow people with a provisional licence to apply for a full licence – even though they had never passed a test.

Daddy had no sense of what to do. He couldn't do the gears and if you ever took a drive with him, you would be scared out of your wits. One day he came home and the whole side of the car was smashed in.

'What happened?'

'A fellow overtook me and hit me.'

'How could a fellow overtake you and hit you on the inside?'

He goes, 'I don't care what you think, that's what happened.'

The joke is that he loved driving, but when he got into the car his whole persona changed. Suddenly he was Stirling Moss.

This might explain why he began to suffer from high blood pressure and had to ease off work. His employers at the newspaper put him on what amounted to half time; he'd finish at two every day, but they didn't cut his wages.

Myself, I knew a car was a passport to freedom. Eventually I got my own car, a Fiat Mirafiori 131. So, now I had a half-decent wage packet, with overtime, and a car, but I still had issues: women.

* * *

I was very shy with them – I didn't know what to do. Looking back, I suppose the problem was because I felt out of control – a throwback to Smyth, who had total control over me. I didn't actually know how to take control and decide what was right and what was wrong, or how to go about it even.

I was passive. Things had been done to me, so with women I was almost afraid to make a move. On top of that I was worried about my sexuality. Being gay was frowned upon, no doubt about that, and after what I had been through I wasn't certain what was going on. At one stage, I was probably about fifteen, I experimented with other boys, touched penises one afternoon. It was a 'you show me yours, I'll show you mine' sort of thing. And though I didn't feel any burst of attraction or excitement, I did wonder if I was odd.

Was I cursed? Hormones were bursting through me at this stage, but I was still confused, as confused as I'd been when puberty hit and Smyth was still around.

There was no one to talk this through with. I couldn't imagine bringing this up with my parents and there were no counsellors that I knew of, so I had to negotiate the way forward purely by instinct.

I'd go to a disco and the other lads might be able to chat someone up and pull a girl. Me, totally different. I relied on getting to know someone, hoping they might even make the first move. I wasn't a complete disaster. There was one girlfriend when I was sixteen, a lovely lass, from the area. And then I met Martina.

The band was going at the time and my sister Moira would bring along this friend of hers called Martina Callan. They were both working in Clarks shoe factory. There were nights when Martina would stay over in our place with my sister, Moira. I was still with my first girlfriend when I met Martina and so she was off limits, but I kept an eye on her just the same.

She was smart and sassy, ready to tell me off if I was talking nonsense. And she was pretty. At first I just noticed her, had her on a far-away radar, but then it got to the stage that I would go home after a night out with my girlfriend and hope Martina would be staying with Moira and that they hadn't gone to sleep yet.

There were lots of late-night chats, innocent chats over tea and biscuits, before I made the decisive move and attempted to kiss her. To my wonderful surprise, she didn't pull away but hugged me close.

Years later, Martina told me that she had sat down with my father one night and told him that she really liked me, but didn't know what to do. Daddy told her to follow her heart – 'If you want him, go get him.'

Next thing she buys me a jumper for my birthday. That was the real start of it. The two us in love and I was feeling really good about it all. The usual foostering about followed. But both sets of parents kept an eye on us. Sex outside marriage was not on, and if you'd been caught, there would have been war.

The Swinging Sixties had come and gone and seemingly forgotten to visit Dundalk. There was no sexual revolution there. There was no contraception; that was banned. Not even condoms. And woe betide the girl who got caught outside of marriage. Any girls who got pregnant were put on the boat over to England to have abortions, or sent away to finish the pregnancy out of sight before the baby was adopted. Few would stay around because of the slur on the name.

Anne and Jimmy got married on 29 September 1979 – the very day that Pope John Paul II said a special mass, just twenty miles away in Drogheda. The hotel asked the couple to postpone their wedding, but this was too much of an ask even for people with a very strong Catholic faith. After all, this was the first Boland wedding in a generation. The wedding mass though was not at midday, as planned, but was moved to ten o'clock so the priest could get to Drogheda and see the Pope.

It was the night after the wedding that Martina and I 'came out' and let everyone know we were an item. One year on and we were engaged ourselves. I was nineteen when I proposed, still serving my time as an apprentice, but I had prospects. Martina was two years younger but far wiser than most her age. She said yes, no doubts at all. Which was a great relief.

*   *   *

Just before this, when we were out one night, I said to Martina, 'I have something to tell you before we get any more serious, before we get engaged. I need you to know something about me.'

This was the moment I decided to tell her about what had happened with Smyth. I didn't want any secrets and maybe I was afraid that some day this would come out. I had told no one else about it, not breathed a word since 1975, though there was no reason for me to worry because there was no sign of Smyth ever coming back into my life.

This wasn't an ordinary secret; this was one that brought with it an element of shame too. And because it was about abuse, sex was also in the mix. I was scared that she would reject me straight out, think that somehow I was responsible for what had happened. But she had to know.

So I told her. 'I was abused.' Then I told her who did it. I told her everything about him, and about the canonical inquiry. I explained that it had been dealt with and that Smyth couldn't harm or attack anyone else. The details of the abuse? I said nothing about that.

There was a pause, for a moment or two, then she put her arms around me and said it meant nothing to her. Utterly irrelevant, she said. We never spoke of it again, not until much later. I had told her my big ugly secret; she had accepted me, so that was it ended.

She's told me since that she'd been terrified of what might be coming, that I was two-timing her, that there were loads of different women. I was working away a lot at the time, so she thought I might have met someone else on the road.

I remember going to Martina's dad and asking him if it was OK if we got engaged. He didn't give the most enthusiastic response, told me to wait. What he was saying basically was that I hadn't the money to marry his daughter, and he was right, but it didn't matter.

We wrote up a note, announcing the deed, left it in Martina's house and off to Dublin with us to buy the ring. Appleby's jewellers it was. There was no fuss when we got back and my own parents were happy enough.

* * *

Martina's dad was proven right. The economy collapsed locally and, before you know it, I was qualified but out of a job. There was no work anywhere, even with my qualifications. I ended up working as a line operator in Clarks Shoes. I was called a cementer. I'd apply glue to the shoe, then it would go down the production line so the next person could put the sole on it. A boring job but there was nothing else going.

And then Clarks shoe factory closed down and I got a job in S and S, an engineering company, making machines that make cardboard boxes. At least I was an electrician there, but, after a year, it closed down too. I was beginning to think it was me. I was a jinx. Everywhere I went, they closed.

Then there was the time of the big gamble in the run up to Christmas in 1981.

Daddy's friend Pat Byrne, from Cullaville in South Armagh, had brought word that his horse couldn't be beat. It was called Carraige and was due to run in the races at Navan, in County Meath, the following week.

Pat Byrne, who my father had got to know through the shows, rarely got these things wrong. He was not the sort to make idle boasts and, as far as my father was concerned, this was a guaranteed win. So off to the races with us, me and Daddy.

I staked £150, all my wages and any savings I had lying around, on the horse. At 16/1. I stood to win more than £2,000. My father never told me how much he put down, but it was certainly a lot more than my bet.

The bookies smiled as they took the money and we smiled back. Then down to the rails for the race itself. It was over jumps, maybe a three-mile chase, and Carraige was flying. Delirium was dripping from us as the horse rounded the last corner with just one to jump. Over, cleanly and in a clear lead. Just the finishing post to pass.

And then the horse stopped. Just like that. Stopped and would go no further. The rest of the field cantered on by and took the prizes. We were left with beaten dockets and long faces. It turned out that, unbeknownst to Pat, Carraige had equine influenza; it recovered and raced again but never with my money on its back.

Daddy has never, to this day, told me how much he had on the horse, but it must have hurt. I was still living at home and I remember the festive season was a little less festive than normal.

My mother took it in her stride. If she was annoyed, she didn't say. This had been my first foray into the gambling world, and I made sure it was my last.

Meanwhile, our own wedding plans were being made. First, in 1981, a home. A three-bedroomed semi-detached at Greenacres in Dundalk, bought with the help of a council loan. We spent the next year and a half doing it up. But there was no co-habiting going on, no way. Astonishing to think how different things are today. We consummated the relationship all right but only by good luck, considering the watchful eye of my father.

Our wedding was planned for September 1983. Before then there was the death of my much-loved grandfather to deal with. The big regret I have was the last time he came round to see me I was sitting watching a favourite programme on television. He stood there talking to me, but I was only interested in the TV, and next thing I remember him saying, 'OK,

I am going home now.' And he went away and the next morning he was in hospital with a stroke, which he never recovered from. He spent the following ten months dying.

I had a job in Limerick at the time, but I left it to be with him. Myself, family and close friends sat up with him every night, for those months, until his death in August that year. There was a mirror situated at the bottom of the stairs, which meant we could keep an eye on him from the living room without disturbing him. Near the end I sat with him most days and nights. One night my mum told me to go and have a break.

I went down to Tom Clark's pub at the Quay. As I was drinking my first pint, a song came on the radio 'Hurry Home' by a band called Wavelength. I thought it was a sign for me to go home but ordered another drink. I went back to find my grandfather had passed away about fifteen minutes earlier.

I wanted to postpone the wedding, which was scheduled for just three weeks later, but my family persuaded us to go ahead. That was right. My grandfather wouldn't have wanted it any other way.

We got married at St Joseph's Redemptorist Church, with the reception in the Derryhale Hotel on the Carrrick Road. That hotel is another economic casualty – well gone. Honeymoon in Majorca. Before long we spent our first married night in our own home, in a proper marital bed. When we woke up the next morning, my father was outside knocking. Jaysus, my first thought was, how do we explain this? We've been caught. I'd forgotten we were married!

* * *

The work situation never steadied. I got one job, then another as the companies closed one after the other. Ireland was in deep trouble then. Young people were leaving in their thousands just as we've seen over the last number of years. My memories of Ireland then are all in black and white, no colour. Except for the kids.

Martina had two tough pregnancies but delivered two beautiful wee boys, first Stephen in 1985 and then Niall in 1988. On both occasions I was the clichéd Irish male, outside the door of the labour ward then off to the pub to wet the baby's head.

The pub became a consolation prize for the absence of work. There was one Christmas we didn't have any Christmas dinner, though we had a fine cake courtesy of Martina's mother. That was before the children arrived. I couldn't go to my father and ask for a loan because I always found enough to go to the pub for a pint. If I had money for a pint, I should have had money for the rest.

By this stage the only people working in Dundalk were in the brewery, the hospital and the council. I exaggerate, a little, but it was impossible to get work. We'd grown up in a town where there always seemed to be plenty of employment, but that era was gone.

The only positive memory I have of that time, apart from Martina and the family, is the Ireland/England football match in the European championships.

That day, Martina, who was heavily pregnant with Niall, went down to her mother's. I went down to O'Connor's Bar on Barrack Street, down to watch the match, and the bar was packed, too packed. There was a big lounge out the back, but no television. So I said, I will sort you out a television. Off I went home, unplugged our own TV, carried it out to a car and back down to the pub and watched the football.

I remember that game and the craic so well. Ray Houghton scored the winner with a header to beat England 1-0. And the place went wild. We were all going mad about football at the time, the first time we'd qualified for a major tournament. And then it was back to reality.

I went out on my own, bought myself a van for £600, but it was costing more to run the van than I was taking in. We were in dire straits; there was no money, no work, and we had two kids. England then came into it.

An uncle there tipped me off about a big electrical contract underway at Stansted Airport, where they were building a new terminal. I applied and, before long, I was helping fit new conveyer belts there. That was February 1989. I went to England first and the family followed at Easter. The money was fine, five maybe six hundred quid a week. Finally, a break. But I was working seven days a week, rarely home, and Martina was going spare with the children and not knowing anyone. She was lonely; I was too busy to be lonely.

Harlow, the town we had moved to, was just south of Stansted Airport, north-east of London. It wasn't a very exciting place, but its saving grace then was a thriving Irish club, The Four Provinces. There had been a big Irish community there, dating back to the 1950s, and we were part of the next generation of emigrants. It is closed now, but it helped us settle. Firm friendships were made there.

Seán and Brigid Whelan are lifelong friends since that time. They had left Ireland for England six months before me. Martina found others in the same boat as herself and that probably kept her from going insane, or home. She made friends with other parents at the local parent/toddler group, in particular with Gill and Tony Tohill. In time all these relationships would be very significant.

Two years later, I applied for and got a job with News International; that's Rupert Murdoch's company, down at Wapping. I've been there ever since, working as an electrical engineer, with the job title of technical support engineer. By coincidence, I had ended up in the newspaper industry, the same as my father.

Our roles are very different. There are no compositors employed in the industry any more; their jobs have been automated, but I do get to watch the presses pump out the newsprint as my father did in his day. By now, he had retired and was trying to mind himself. He never drank but he did smoke, the untipped variety, Sweet Afton, and he ended up with a triple by-pass heart operation. He gave up the fags there and then.

My own job involves helping supervise the running of the printing operation. There are twelve machines, each capable of printing 86,000 copies an hour. Nothing can interrupt the presses once they have started a run, and it's my job to make sure that any faults are fixed just about immediately. It is a pressurised environment because time really is money in this business, but I enjoy it there; I have good friends, good conditions and good craic too.

* * *

The financial side of things was now sorted. We got ourselves a nice home, nothing fancy but it suited our needs, and our focus became the two boys. They were coming along fine, but there was one telling incident.

We had Stephen in the local Catholic school and naturally expected him to make his Communion there. Now that we had children, we were both going to mass regularly, as much for the boys as for ourselves. But because of my shift work, we went to a neighbouring parish for mass on Saturday evenings at seven.

Out of the blue, we got a message from the local priest saying that Stephen wasn't going to be allowed make his Communion with his class. The priest had decided that there was no evidence that the wee lad was attending mass in his parish, and so Stephen couldn't take his Communion.

You can imagine the response in our home when this flared up.

I challenged the priest, 'You are telling me you are going to refuse him make his first Holy Communion with all his classmates, who he plays football with, who he runs around the school yard with?'

'Yes,' he says. 'He doesn't go to mass.'

I lost it. I swore at him. And I explained, between curses, that he did attend. But there was no convincing him.

I said, fair enough. Then I went home and wrote a letter to the Bishop. That sorted it. Stephen was allowed to make his Communion. I was so furious because of all I had been through. I definitely took it personally because by now I had a well-tuned antennae to figure priests out. Some go about with the arrogance of the Church shining through them.

You'd think that such priests were my main concern when Stephen came home one day and said he wanted to become an altar boy. You'd be right, but, of course, there was more to it. Stephen had no idea what bomb he was detonating when he announced his plans to go on the altar. He was shocked when I snapped back, 'Certainly not, Stephen.' He wanted an explanation, but I wasn't going to say anything at that stage, so I just told him 'No', and that was the end of the discussion.

In fact, I wasn't just worried about my children being attacked by a priest, I was worried about leaving them alone in any adult company, or under the supervision of any adult. So when they decided they wanted to join the boy scouts, the cubs, go on school trips, after-school activity clubs, I stopped all that too.

I was afraid of any male in charge of children. Martina and I didn't even discuss this, because she understood the issues too. She had started working at a children's nursery and couldn't have been more conscious of the need to protect our boys. Remember too, that the boys were both coming up to the age that I had been abused.

Naturally, Stephen spotted something was different between our attitude and that of other parents; he was that few years older than Niall. He was annoyed and wanted to know 'why I was ruining his life'. I told him that I would tell him some day when he was bigger, when he was older.

Football was different. I let them play football because I could be there when they were playing; I could be there when they were training. I got involved in the club as a fundraiser as well. I was there all the time, and when I wasn't there, because of my work shifts, Martina was. Both boys loved their football, and were good at it. They played for the county school teams.

I was constantly afraid of leaving the children in the care of others. Exceptions were made for certain babysitters. When we went out, we would go to the Garden Tiger which was our local, just a few hundred yards from home. We became very friendly with the owners, Mick and Sylvie Wisbey. The boys would call them Uncle Mick and Auntie Sylvie. They had a daughter called Nicola. She was a young teenager who would babysit the boys upstairs while Martina and I enjoyed ourselves in the bar. I knew she wasn't a threat to the boys. Nicola then became our babysitter for the next few years, giving us the freedom to enjoy ourselves, knowing that Stephen and Niall were safe. This was the first time we let anyone other than family members look after Stephen and Niall.

The daughters of our good friends Seán and Brigid Whelan were also trusted. Karen and Noleen were in their mid-teens at the time, and again they were no threat to the boys. The boys loved when we went out – I suppose they enjoyed the freedom and fun they had with the girls.

Did the boys lose out? Yes, I feel badly about it now but I only knew what life had thrown up at us: Smyth.

It was 1994 when Smyth came back, centre stage, into my life. My sister Eilish phoned. I'd let the sisters in on the secret years before, in the one and only conversation I had with them about it. She'd heard news of a documentary on television about Smyth, saying he had abused children all over the world and was now in prison in Northern Ireland. She had taped it and promised to send it over. In those times there wasn't the internet. I had to wait until the tape landed through the letterbox and then we watched it.

Chapter 8
The Past Comes Back

We got the tape sometime in October 1994. The television programme, *Suffer Little Children* by Chris Moore, was devastating. That was when I learned about Smyth's abuse in America, in Britain and up and down Ireland, much of it after 1975. I had no idea of the scale of the abuse.

I suppose like many victims of abuse you think it is confined to your little world. I know of one family where one brother was abused, then another and finally a third. These boys only discovered that their siblings had been abused when the police began an investigation years later.

I couldn't believe it. It was like being hit with a bus. Jesus, me thinking he was supposed to have been dealt with in 1975 and here he was now in prison for abusing children, some of whom were only just born back then. I was in a total spin. I had myself convinced that I had sorted him out. That he could never upset a child again.

I was living proof of the damage that his abuse caused. He had left me with a permanent scar, though he had never hit me. I was secure in my sexuality, but sex itself was often tainted by the memory of that first sexual experience.

You know when you hear of people saying about how lovely their first sexual experience was, or how exciting it was, well, mine wasn't. And there was nothing I could ever do to undo it. Martina and I worked it out, but there were times when all I could see was him. What consoled me was that I had brought an end to him. And then it turned out I hadn't.

* * *

The television programme affected Martina too. After what we'd been through, I am sure she was worried that this would raise issues for me again. She was right. My parents were in bits themselves; they felt haunted by the man.

From the documentary I learned that in June that year Smyth had been convicted in Belfast of 17 charges of abuse against 5 girls and 2 boys over a period dating from 1964 to 1988. 1988 ... That date jumped out at me. That was years after I had taken part in the canonical inquiry.

The programme outlined decades of abuse, how it was well known to the Church, in particular to Smyth's order, and how it had been covered up. From 1979 Smyth had spent two years in North Dakota, USA; one former altar boy there was paid $20,000 by Smyth. But the story began much earlier.

Investigative journalist Chris Moore detailed the suspicions, the rumours, the allegations and the facts, going all the way back to the 1940s. Documents that have come my way since have also enlightened me. The point is the Church authorities appear to have been aware of his criminality from almost the start.

Fr Brendan Smyth was born in 1927. His baptismal name was John Gerard. One of three children raised in a terraced house off the Falls Road in west Belfast, he went to a local Christian Brothers school. In his teenage years he was known to some of his friends as 'The Fiddler', according to Chris Moore, who later wrote a book, *Betrayal of Trust*, about Smyth.

The Second World War had just ended, in September 1945, when Smyth was vested in the Norbertine Order at Holy Trinity Abbey, Kilnacrott, County Cavan.

He was eighteen and considered smart enough to be encouraged to go to Rome to study.

He attended the illustrious Gregorian University, right in the centre of the city. Rome was still reeling in the immediate aftermath of the Second World War. It must have been in total chaos at the time with many opportunities for someone like Smyth to act out his deviancy. Rumours that he had misbehaved in some shadowy and dark way followed him back to Cavan when he was ordained in 1951.

In 1964 one Norbertine priest, Fr Bruno Mulvihill, heard these rumours shortly after he arrived at Kilna-crott as a novice.

Thirty-one years later, in 1995, Fr Mulvihill was to tell investigating gardaí that he and another priest had been walking the grounds of the abbey when they'd heard the cries and sobs of children from an adjacent building. He described how he wasn't able to see where the sounds were coming from but reported that his colleague 'enlightened me as to the nature of the matter'.

Fr Mulvihill had then learned that there were rumours about Smyth and child abuse going back to the late 1940s. The two went to see Abbot Colwell, who was in charge of the abbey, and reported what they had heard, but Fr Mulvihill claimed they were met with a rebuff. Within months Smyth was on his way to a parish in Providence, Rhode Island, on the east coast of America.

Fr Smyth spent the next three years there. One morning, in early 1968, Fr Mulvihill answered a phone call to Kilnacrott. It was the Bishop of Providence, Russell McVinney, asking for the Abbot. The Abbot was ill in hospital, so Fr Mulvihill took a message.

Fr Mulvihill reported that he was told that Smyth was flying home from the US. He said he was told that Smyth's appointment had been terminated because of a 'sexual misdemeanour'.

Fr Mulvihill later learned that Smyth had already been sent home from two other postings, from Scotland and Wales, years earlier, because of 'trouble with juveniles'.

All of this is down in black and white in Fr Mulvihill's statement to the gardaí, which he made almost thirty years later. The next development that transpired that same summer of 1968 was even more extraordinary. Fr Mulvihill reported that he found a formal notification from the Congregation of the Religious in Rome instructing that Smyth was not to leave the precincts of the Abbey unless under the supervision of another priest and that his faculties for

Confession were to be withdrawn for life. Fr Mulvi-hill said he had found this in a drawer in a room that Smyth had used.

He claimed to have reported this to the senior cleric in charge, who assured him the document would be placed in Smyth's file. This document has not turned up since. Later the Church would say they have no record of it or of any action being taken by the Congre-gation of the Religious. But a letter from the Bishop of Providence has turned up. And it is, in my opinion, a masterpiece of clerical bullshit.

The letter, dated 15 February, is written to Abbot Cowell. It begins:

> I regret to have to inform you that I have sent Father Brendan Smyth home. I was under the impression that he was doing very well in the parish to which he was assigned. To my amazement it is now reported to me that he doesn't measure up on several counts.
>
> His rapport with the adult parishioners has not been happy. He seemed dedicated enough to the young people, and in some cases too much. So, we feel that for the good of the parish and the souls and for his own sake he should return to his Monastery.

February 15, 1968

Rt. Rev. Abbot Felim C. Colwell, C.R.P.
Holy Trinity Abbey
Kilnacrott, Ballyjamesduff
County Cavan, Ireland

Dear Abbot Colwell:

I regret to have to inform you that I have sent Father Brendan
Smyth home. I was under the impression that he was doing
very well in the parish to which he was assigned. To my
amazement it is now reported to me that he doesn't measure
up on several counts. His rapport with the adult parishioners
has not been happy. He seemed dedicated enough to the
young people, and in some cases too much. So, we feel that
for the good of the parish and the souls and for his own sake
he should return to his Monastery.

He had already planned to go back to Ireland within a couple
of weeks. I told him to remain at his post until he had made
definite arrangements to depart and once in Ireland not to plan
to return.

I am sorry to have to share this disappointment with you, but
I hope that you are getting on well.

With assurance of my continuing esteem, I am

Sincerely yours in Christ,

Bishop of Providence

*The Bishop of Providence writes to Brendan Smyth's superiors
saying he has to send him home to Ireland; 'He seemed dedicated
enough to the young people, and in some cases too much.'*

Thus, Fr Smyth was sent home to carry on where he had left off. The fact of the matter is that he had abused children in the parish of New Greenwich, Rhode Island. I have since met one of his victims there, Helen McGonigle. She and her sister were abused. Helen was six years old. There were others. The Church knew but simply moved the culprit on. Parents were not told. This pattern would become clear to me much later. Abbot Cowell died at the end of 1968. If he had lived, maybe things would have been different.

The authorities at Kilnacrott kept quiet, but they did send Fr Smyth for aversion therapy at a psychiatric hospital in Belfast. It made no difference. The only way to stop this man was to go to the proper authorities, the police, but this was never done.

Kilnacrottt was next door to the town of Ballyjamesduff. It's famous for a Percy French song, 'Come Back Paddy Reilly, to Ballyjamesduff'.

Various investigations would later prove that Fr Smyth was abusing children in the area from the 1950s. Some of them were cajoled into helping him in his fund-raising efforts, organising the envelopes, making sure the addresses were correct, sealing them – the sort of odd jobs that children could manage without supervision.

Of course there was one supervisor – himself. And so children were abused. I know that one woman reported being raped by him at the age of ten. He took her into a room, locked the door and pocketed the key. The amazing thing was exactly how much freedom he had. Unless he was assigned to a specific parish, as he was in Rhode Island, he had no particular job or ministry. This meant he was floating around the place, filling in here and there. He wasn't one to waste his time; he was in and out of houses, of schools and orphanages. His favourite tactic was to ask to see a specific child, alone and in private. Then he would assault them.

Fr Mulvihill, meanwhile, had not forgotten about what he knew. He had been based abroad but he returned each year, for two or three months at a time. In 1970 he reported seeing Smyth driving a Northern Ireland registered car. He recalled the document he had seen forbidding Fr Smyth from leaving Kilnacrott alone. Fr Mulvihill attempted to raise the matter with the new Abbot, Kevin Smith.

According to Fr Mulvihill, the Abbot told him that Fr Smyth had suffered enough. The Abbot reportedly said that he had spoken to Fr Smyth, who assured him that there would be no further misdemeanour. But then Fr Mulvihill saw another child, sobbing, leaving a storeroom in Smyth's company. Later, a boy – aged ten or thereabouts – went to Fr Mulvihill and said: 'Fr Smyth stuck his hand up my arse again.'

All this Fr Mulvihill says he reported to Abbot Smith. And when he did, Fr Mulvihill says he was told that he must be of similar sexual orientation to Fr Smyth to notice all these things.

In his witness statement to gardaí, in 1995, Fr Bruno Mulvihill claimed to have reported his concerns about Fr Brendan Smyth to the Papal Nuncio, Archbishop Alibrandi. The great and the good of the Church had gathered at Kilnacrott, in the summer of 1974, to celebrate the fiftieth anniversary of the arrival of the Order in Ireland. None of the guests were more eminent than the Pope's personal emissary to Ireland, the Papal Nuncio, Archbishop Alibrandi.

According to Fr Mulvihill's statement, the Archbishop was told of the possibility of an impending scandal of 'unforeseeable dimensions' if Fr Smyth wasn't dealt with properly. Fr Mulvihill said he also spoke directly to the Bishop of Kilmore, Francis McKiernan, about Smyth. He claimed that the Bishop showed no interest in the complaint, nor did the Papal

Nuncio. Fr Mulvihill says he followed up the conversations with letters to both prelates.

We know now that Fr Brendan Smyth was sent for treatment to England that year, the third time he'd been sent away. I can testify to its ineffectiveness. This was at the same time as I was being abused.

His abbot, Kevin Smith, admitted that he believed Smyth's problems with children surfaced shortly after he began his religious life. He told Chris Moore: 'Father Smyth was reassigned every few years or so in an effort to keep him from forming attachments to families and their children. We now see how inadequate this approach actually was.'

He'd been sent away for treatment at least three times, but it never stopped him offending. This man was dangerous; the Church knew it and failed to stop him. They tried to claim credit for sending him for treatment, but they knew this treatment was having no impact, so why didn't they take more drastic steps?

There was so much that was outrageous in the behaviour of the religious authorities that I couldn't be astonished when I learned that, as late as 1990, Smyth been appointed, with the backing of his abbot, as part-time chaplin to Tralee hospital in Kerry.

Abbot Kevin Smith resigned his post a few days after the documentary broadcast. The programme had revealed that the Church knew about Smyth and his paedophile tendencies for a very long time. It also raised one other matter, a delay in the extradition of Smyth from the Irish Republic to the authorities in Northern Ireland. It turned out that he'd been working as the part-time hospital chaplin in Tralee, County Kerry, even as the police in Northern Ireland waited for the Dublin authorities to extradite him. There had been a seven-month delay in processing the warrant. Although Smyth was eventually convicted and jailed in Northern Ireland, the issues would prove catastrophic for the ruling coalition government in Dublin, in particular Taoiseach Albert Reynolds. A row over the reasons for the delay led, one way or another, to the collapse of the Fianna Fáil/Labour government. They had overseen the Peace Process and there were worries it would be affected.

* * *

Just about the only detail missing in the television documentary was my involvement in the 1975 canonical inquiry.

I didn't do anything straight away. There was a piece in the local paper at home, which mentioned

Smyth and his abuse in the North, but said there were no known cases in the Louth area. My father, who was up to his limit at this point, read this and he rang the gardaí and said the paper had it wrong. He told them that I had been abused and said that it was supposed to have been dealt with after a tribunal, back in 1975. The funny thing is he never told me that he had gone to the Guards. I only learned that when I got a call from an investigating policeman at the Dundalk station.

* * *

Martina's father had died in October 1994 and we intended to spend Christmas with her mother, so I arranged to speak to the Guards over that time. On 17 December I landed home, and the following evening went up to the station to make my statement. I had no idea how long it would take, but it took hours.

I started talking at nine and finished shortly before four o'clock in the morning. They were all up awake in Martina's mother's house when I got back, wondering how it went. It had been very draining, physically and emotionally. I can remember being exhausted afterwards, not that the Guard was tough or sceptical, or anything like that; in fact he was very sympathetic. But this process was difficult for me, resurrecting my memories and going through all the ugly details again.

The statement is six pages long. And in many respects differs very little from the testimony recorded at the Dominican Priory in 1975. But, looking at it now, two things jump out.

One: I had completely forgotten that I had given the canonical inquiry the names and the addresses of the other children who were abused or who were at risk of abuse.

And two: I did name two of the three priests there, Fr Donnelly and Fr McShane, but I was confused about who the third person was. In the statement I refer to him as a 'monsignor', and suggest he was Cardinal Cahal Daly. Of course Cardinal Daly had nothing to do with what happened in 1975.

My father also spoke to the Guards, the following month. Again, he couldn't recall who the third priest was. He thought that he was a monsignor from the archdiocese of Armagh, but he couldn't recall a name.

Cardinal Cahal Daly, who was considered very able and intelligent, had headed the Irish Church from 1990. He was already seventy-three when he took up the post and must have aged rapidly with the pressure that was heaped on him by the Smyth case.

Chris Moore's programme had revealed that the family of at least one other Smyth victim had contacted Cardinal Daly directly years earlier when he had been the Bishop of Down and Connor, the diocese covering Belfast and the second most populous diocese in Ireland.

Some weeks after the broadcast, on 5 December, Cardinal Daly issued a formal statement, most of which is reproduced here:

The conviction of Father Brendan Smyth in June 1994 and the information which has since come to light have given rise to grave and justified public concern. I am profoundly sorry that the crimes of a priest have caused such appalling suffering. I am further anguished that this misconduct was permitted to continue over such a long period of time. The wrong done to the victims and families is all the more cruel because it is a betrayal of the trust which they placed in a priest ordained to minister in the name of Christ. The wrong is not a past event. It may have long-lasting effects on the innocent victims' lives.

I was Bishop of the diocese of Down and Connor from October 1982 until December 1990. ...

On 23rd February 1990 a client, accompanied by a parent, visited the offices of the Catholic Family Welfare Society in Belfast. They were interviewed by one of the Society's social workers. The client told the social worker about sexual abuses suffered at the hands of Father Brendan Smyth over a period of years. The social worker offered advice. She obtained the family's permission to inform the RUC and she did, in fact, report the allegations to the police. She also urged the family themselves to inform the RUC. Subsequently the social worker informed the statutory health and social services authorities.

The social worker also informed the priest Director of the Catholic Family Welfare Society (a priest of the diocese of Down and Connor), who in turn informed my priest secretary. My secretary immediately informed me. I approved of the steps taken and, specifically, expressed my approval of the fact that the allegations had been reported to the police.

On 7th March 1990 a formal statement of complaint was made to the RUC by a member of the same family. Within the next two to three weeks thereafter statements were made to the RUC by other members of the family.

As soon as I was informed about the complaints, I telephoned Father Smyth's religious superior, Abbot Kevin Smith, who alone had ecclesiastical jurisdiction over him. Because of the gravity of the matters reported to me, I sought a meeting with the abbot. The meeting took place on 12th March 1990. I informed the abbot about the complaints. I told him that a social worker had seen the client and that the allegations of abuse had been reported to the RUC. The abbot accepted full responsibility for Father Smyth and undertook to take prompt and appropriate steps to deal with the matter. ...

I left Down and Connor in December 1990, having been appointed Archbishop of Armagh.

In February 1991, by which time I had gone to Armagh, I was contacted by the same family about the matter. I immediately contacted the abbot again, drawing his attention once more to the complaints of the family and strongly emphasising the need for him to take firm action to deal with Father Brendan Smyth. I also telephoned the parish priest of the parish in Belfast where the family lived and requested that he offer pastoral support.

The abbot wrote to me on 21st February 1991. He told me that Father Brendan Smyth had denied that there had been 'any incident of that nature for a couple of years now' and that Father Smyth 'only goes to Belfast to visit his doctor, and otherwise only visits his own family'.

At or about this time I learned that the police investigations, which had commenced in March 1990, were approaching some conclusion and that Court action was anticipated. I now understand that on 8th March 1991 Father Brendan Smyth presented himself for interview by the RUC in connection with these complaints and made admissions of wrongdoing.

In August 1992, the family wrote to me again. They expressed their distress that Father Brendan Smyth had been seen in their district. Once more I communicated with Abbot Smith. I expressed to him my grave and urgent concern at the continuing failure to deal effectively with the problem in spite of firm assurances given to me in 1990 and in 1991. At this time I again telephoned the family's parish priest.

In October 1993 the family made further contact by telephone with my office in Armagh. I understand that, following these telephone calls to my office, the family, as requested by my secretary, made contact with the diocesan offices in Down and Connor. ...

At no time was I aware nor was I made aware of Father Brendan Smyth's long previous history of paedophile crimes. This history became known to me only through the media this year.

As Archbishop of Armagh, as Primate or as Cardinal I have no jurisdiction under canon law or otherwise over any other bishop or diocese or over any priest except the diocesan clergy of the Archdiocese of Armagh and the religious priests of the archdiocese as and when they exercise a pastoral ministry at my appointment in the archdiocese. I have never had any jurisdiction at any time over Father Brendan Smyth.

Chris Moore tells me that Cardinal Daly has underplayed his influence and involvement over Smyth. Canon law expert Fr Tom Doyle told me that the prelate was, at the very least, terribly mistaken about the remit of his power. Speaking personally, I think Cardinal Daly was completely ineffectual. Smyth was free to continue to abuse children long after Cardinal Daly had first been notified about him. A pattern was emerging.

Five days after this statement, Rome announced that Cardinal Daly, then seventy-nine, was stepping down. That was not terribly surprising, but the choice of his successor was.

On 13 December 1994 Pope John Paul II announced that Monsignor Seán Brady was being appointed the Coadjutor Archbishop of Armagh, essentially the heir apparent to Cardinal Daly.

That was five days before I sat down in Dundalk Garda Station. It was in all the papers and the media at the time and I must have had some subliminal memory of his name but confused him with Cardinal Daly.

* * *

Cardinal Seán Brady was born in 1939 and grew up in the rural parish of Laragh, County Cavan. Ordained in 1964, he earned a doctorate in Canon Law at the Pontifical Lateran University in Rome three years later. Afterwards, he taught in St Patrick's College in Cavan until 1980. He combined his teaching role there with his post as part-time secretary to the Bishop of Kilmore.

He was assigned to the Irish Pontifical College in Rome from 1980 and became rector there in 1987. He was dispatched back to Ireland, in 1993, where he spent a year in the Cavan parish of Ballyhaise and was then known as Monsignor Seán Brady. Then came that big promotion.

It wasn't just me and my father who couldn't recall his name from the 1975 inquiry. In 1982 Oliver McShane had left the priesthood and was living, happily married, in London. The gardaí contacted him after my father's phone call. When he was interviewed, he too couldn't recall the name of the third priest, but he clarified that it was a canon lawyer from the diocese of Kilmore.

He told investigators the background to the canonical inquiry and explained how he had been contacted by Bishop McKiernan following the inquiry. The Bishop told him that Smyth had been dealt with and said that he wanted to reassure him that this would not happen again. He also told McShane how, as a result of the information that I had given, a number of other boys had been discovered who had been similarly abused by Smyth. Just like me and my father, Oliver McShane had been told Smyth would be dealt with and that children were safe.

By this time, Fr Francis Donnelly had become a monsignor. He was also interviewed by gardaí but declined to make a written statement. He said his recollection was quite vague, but a memo of the interview was taken by the investigating garda.

According to the Garda memo, Monsignor Donnelly recalled interviewing a boy, 'possibly Brendan Boland', at the priory. He explained to the garda:

'His [Donnelly's] role was that of recording secretary, ie he made a record of the questions and answers, and when the interview was over he handed the document to the Priest in Charge [sic], who was a Monsignor, he could not recall the name of the Monsignor.'

Monsignor Donnelly's memory is flawed. The transcripts make it clear that it was he who asked the questions. Although I remember Fr Brady, as he was then, asking one or two questions, these may have been in the form of supplementary questions. And it was Fr Brady who took the notes. Monsignor Donnelly also says that the other monsignor – referring to Cardinal Brady – was the 'Priest in Charge'.

Monsignor Donnelly's interview took place in February 1995, three months after Monsignor Brady had been appointed as Monsignor Donnelly's boss, or technically, his boss-in-waiting.

The Garda memo continued:

'He [Donnelly] did not speak to the Father of the injured party at any time. He could recall that the injured party allowed the alleged culprit (Fr Smith) [sic] with his parents' consent up to his bedroom to

Memo of Interview with Monsignor Francis Donnelly at Parochial House, St. Patricks Cathedral on 15th February 1995 with Sergeant L. Witherow, 18502G.

I interviewed Monsignor Frank Donnelly re alleged complaint by ▇▇▇▇▇▇▇▇ formerly of ▇▇▇▇▇▇▇▇▇▇▇▇▇▇ who alleged that he was sexually abused by a Fr. Brendan Smith, Kilnacrott Abbey in 1971. Monsignor Donnelly declined to make a written statement, he said that his recollection was quite vague. He could recall interviewing a boy possibly▇▇▇▇▇▇ ▇▇▇▇ at the Friary, Dundalk about 24 years ago. His role was that of recording secretary, i.e. he made a record of questions and answers and when the interview was over he handed the document over to the Priest in Charge, who was a Monsignor, he could not recall the name of the Monsignor. He stated that the number of Clergy present would be 3 maybe 4. He did not speak to▇▇▇▇▇▇▇▇ Father of the injured party at any time. He could recall that the injured party allowed the alleged culprit (Fr. Smith) with his parents consent up to his bedroom to discuss vocations. Monsignor Donnelly stated that he was not happy with the interview of the young boy as he thought some of the answers were a bit woolly. He also stated that he had checked at Arus Coell in Armagh and there was no record of the interview at the Friary in Dundalk, which would indicate that the Church Authorities may not have attached much significance to these allegations.

A copy of the original Garda memo of the interview with Monsignor Francis Donnelly. According to the garda, he declined to make a written statement.

discuss vocations. Monsignor Donnelly stated that he was not happy with the interview of the young boy as he thought some of his answers were woolly.'

Some of my answers were 'woolly'? My answers were direct and straight to the point.

I have spoken to the Garda officer who took most of these statements; his name is Larry Witherow. He's retired now, but when I told him that I was writing this book he agreed to help me with some fact checking. I asked him if he had ever discovered who the third priest was; he hadn't back then. The involvement of Cardinal Brady only became clear to him through my court case much later.

My main question: was Cardinal Brady interviewed about Smyth as part of his investigation? He told me that, to the best of his knowledge, Cardinal Brady was not interviewed.

I then asked him, if he had known about Cardinal Brady's involvement (ie that he was the third priest at the inquiry), would he have wanted to speak to him? He said, 'Most definitely.'

Larry Witherow cannot discount the possibility that another officer spoke to Cardinal Brady, though he doubts it.

* * *

In the 1990s there was only one oblique public reference to my canonical inquiry.

In October 1995 Bishop McKiernan admitted he had known about Smyth's abuse back in 1975. This is what he told RTÉ:

'Complaints were made to me at that time. And I had those complaints investigated. I found that they were substantiated, as far as I could see that they were true and I reported the matter to the Abbot at Kilnacrott at the time and took away Fr Smyth's faculties to hear Confession.'

It is remarkable for what he doesn't say as much as for what he says.

He says nothing about a formal canonical inquiry, nothing about who took part, nothing about who was involved in the inquiry and nothing about all the information that the Church had been given.

This pattern of revealing only the most limited information was completely characteristic of how the Church dealt with the whole controversy. 'The truth, nothing but the whole truth' – Jaysus.

* * *

All the anxiety, anger and frustration that bubbled away in me over the years was now at the surface. There were nights I couldn't sleep. Nights when I did sleep but I woke up in sweats. Drinking became a bit of an issue. I did go to a Dundalk solicitor and spoke about taking on the Church in a civil suit, but I was left in no doubt that the firm concerned had no interest in taking the case. The Church and its priests were a protected species, though it was clear to me that the gardaí were keen on a prosecution through the criminal courts.

All through this time Smyth was very much in the public eye. There were reports that he was being attacked in Magilligan Prison, where he was serving his sentence in Northern Ireland. Prisoners had urinated on his bed and thrown excrement at him. I didn't rejoice in that but I understood why inmates might want to hurt or humiliate him.

Newspapers reported that, despite these problems, he'd apparently adapted well to prison life with a routine of reading, praying and the opportunity to say mass daily. Sources told one paper that he received donations from well-wishers totalling several thousand pounds.

The climate was changing. People who had buried their abuse in shame and in fear of the power of the clergy were now coming forward. In September 1995 there was a second court case in Belfast. Again Smyth admitted the offences. This time there were 13 children involved, 9 girls and 4 boys, who were abused between 1969 and 1988. He received a further three years in jail. These cases were confined to abuse which had occurred within Northern Ireland, but because Smyth's abuse was so prolific there were many victims. My own case was still to come up in the Dublin courts, but it would have to wait until Smyth was in a position to face trial, until he had served his sentences in the North.

* * *

I was numb at this point. Martina was having to cope with me and finding it difficult because I wasn't the sort to open up and talk about my feelings. When she asked me to sit down and talk, my first response was to get up and leave the house. Off to the pub. There had been a conscious decision, of sorts, never to talk about it after I had revealed to her what had gone on before we were engaged. As the years passed, it had receded into the background, but now it was staring me down again. And worse was the feeling that I had been given the opportunity to sort him out back in 1975 but had failed.

The thing is, when you look back, you don't imagine yourself as a terrified fourteen-year-old. You look back as an adult and wonder what you should have done. The same with the abuse itself. You see pictures of Smyth as an old man, in his sixties, and you wonder how on earth you let him near you all those years ago. You don't factor in that you were just a kid, and that he was a powerful, big man with his bags of sweets, manipulating you into submission. Your perspective is all skewed. You are thinking about it all from the perspective of an adult.

Phone calls were coming, day in, day out, from the Director of Public Prosecutions (DPP) in Dublin, or from the gardaí. With every phone call there were always more questions. I thought, I am sick of this. I have had enough of this probing. How many times have I got to go through this? Do you not believe me? How many times do I have to explain myself?

I couldn't get away from it. I was going insane.

* * *

Somehow, through Martina, we made contact with Oliver McShane. That was the smartest thing we ever did. We arranged to go and visit him in London, where he was living with his wife and family. This was the first time I had seen him since 1975.

It was powerful, to meet somebody who knew

what had happened and who believed me totally. No questions. It turned into a great visit. His children were much the same ages as our own; everyone was entertained. And the two of us took time out for a long walk, which allowed me to get a lot off my chest.

He was the first person who really understood what I was going through because he had been there when the evidence had first been heard all those years earlier. I knew immediately that this man could be trusted and that he was on my side. And he had his own extraordinary tale to tell, of how he had discovered that Brendan Smyth continued to have access to children.

He had been in Dublin Airport, waiting for a flight to London, in the summer of 1981 or 1982, when, reading over the shoulder of another traveller, he spotted a picture of Smyth in an evening paper. He bought a copy of the paper and scrutinised the photo: the priest was surrounded by children. The paper reported how he was taking them away from an inner-city Dublin parish to the abbey at Kilnacrott for a holiday.

He thought to himself, Jesus, they did nothing. And, at the same time, he thought that that couldn't be possible. The Bishop had told him Smyth had been sorted.

My protector was in the process of leaving the Church at that time, getting laicised. He was no longer living in Ireland. It wasn't a conscious decision but, having seen the paper, he didn't take it any further, just consigned it to his memory. He has since spoken of how he regrets not having done more.

It seems that no children were safe where Fr Brendan Smyth was concerned. He'd abused them in orphanages, in schools, in churches, in family homes, in libraries, in fields – everywhere. And the same in America.

At the end of that first trial in Belfast, in 1994, Smyth's lawyer told the court that the priest realised he was a 'fixated paedophile' who could not control his urges.

In 1995, during his second court case, Smyth issued a statement saying:

I would like to take this opportunity to express my deep sorrow to anyone who has suffered in any way from my actions and also to their relatives, friends and also members of my religious community who suffered because of the media treatment of these matters. For a long time now I have been at peace with my God and I trust that they too will find a similar peace.

On the face of it, an apology, if a mealy-mouthed one. But that apology did not reflect what Smyth thought. To understand what he was really thinking, we need to turn to the contents of a letter he wrote to Cardinal Daly on 6 December 1994, the day after Cardinal Daly's lengthy statement admitting that he'd first been told about Smyth's tendencies in 1990.

Smyth's letter is shocking and revealing from the very first sentence:

Eminence,

It has been drawn to my attention that you recently stated: 'Fr Brendan Smyth has done serious damage to the Church.' If you have been misquoted then please ignore this letter and destroy it. If you have not been misquoted then I wish to express my anger and disbelief that a person with your lofty intellectual qualifications could possibly have made such a statement.

Whatever my sins and failings – and they are many – it is not they, but the media reporting of them, which has created an atmosphere of mixed shame and embarrassment for the superficial Catholic. And, need I say it, I did not in any way create or encourage the media extravaganza, rather

Standard Aok 6.12.94

In replying to this letter, please address the envelope as follows :

Full Name _B.2769 JOHN G. SMYTH_

Full Address _H1B H.M.P. MAGILLIGAN_

POINT ROAD, MAGILLIGAN

BT 49 OLR

N. IRELAND

2ᵈ SUNDAY OF ADVENTH

EMINENCE,

IT HAS BEEN DRAWN TO MY ATTENTION THAT YOU
RECENTLY STATED: 'FR. BRENDAN SMYTH HAS DONE SERIOUS
DAMAGE TO THE CHURCH'. IF YOU HAVE BEEN MISQUOTED
THEN PLEASE IGNORE THIS LETTER AND DESTROY IT. IF YOU HAVE
NOT BEEN MISQUOTED THEN I WISH TO EXPRESS MY ANGER
AND DISBELIEF THAT A PERSON WITH YOUR LOFTY INTELLECTUAL
QUALIFICATIONS COULD POSSIBLY HAVE MADE SUCH A STATEMENT.
WHATEVER MY SINS AND FAILINGS — AND THEY ARE MANY — IT IS NOT
THEY, BUT THE MEDIA REPORTING OF THEM, WHICH HAS

created an atmosphere of mixed shame and embarrassment for the superficial Catholic. And, need I say it, I did not in any way create or encourage the media extravaganza, rather the contrary. I pleaded "Guilty" to wildly exaggerated and, in some instances, false charges, to try to limit media coverage. In that, I admit, I failed dismally. As a *heartily* *inbred* Catholic Christian I do not believe that it is possible for anyone to damage the Church. The Church is God's gift to His People and He remains ever with it to the end of time, preserving it from all harm. The present unsavoury tempest is a testing, trying, proving experience from which the Church will emerge renewed and (if possible) strengthened.

It is not necessary to answer this letter. A note from a secretary stating that it has been received will suffice.

Respectfully in Christ,

Brendan G. Smyth, *o.praem.*

Fr Brendan Smyth's letter to Cardinal Daly has not been published before. Smyth apologised to his victims in public but this private letter shows little remorse.

the contrary. I pleaded "guilty" to wildly exaggerated and, in some instances, false charges, to try to limit media coverage. In that, I admit, I failed dismally.

As a moderately informed Catholic Christian I do not believe that it is possible for <u>anyone</u> to damage the Church. The Church is God's gift to his people and He remains ever with it to the end of time, preserving it from <u>all</u> harm. The present unsavoury tempest is a testing, trying, proving experience from which the Church will emerge renewed and (if possible) strengthened.

Help me out. Can you see any sign of contrition?

Chapter 9
The Truth Will Out

If you take a look back at Ireland in the 1990s, there was so much going on in terms of the Church and the believers. The believers were starting to thin out a wee bit. Living in England, I missed some of the drama, the debates taking place on the Gay Byrne radio show, or whatever, and some of the referendums on divorce and abortion. But I had heard all about the Bishop of Galway, Eamon Casey, who we learned, in 1992, had fathered a child. And then a year or so later came the story of how Fr Michael Cleary, 'The Singing Priest', had fathered two children.

Isn't it an extraordinary coincidence that they were the two men who performed the roles of MC at the Papal youth mass in Galway in 1979? It seems that most of Ireland managed to get to see Pope John Paul II on his Irish tour, the first papal visit to Ireland. That youth mass was intended to revitalise the Church. I remember busloads of mates leaving Dundalk for the run to Galway. I didn't go, being too caught up with my sister Anne's wedding. It must have devastated the Church hierarchy that these two popular clerics had proven so human and fallible, in respect of sexual sin.

As far as I was concerned, whatever they did, they did what was, at least, natural. They had either fallen in love or succumbed to earthly desires. However, these were normal human instincts, not the desires of predatory child abusers. The problem the Church had in Ireland, it seemed to me, was that it was preoccupied with sexual sins. Or at least sexual sins with women.

I was going through a difficult phase myself. The whole resurrection of the abuse was deeply disturbing for me, as much as I was looking forward to my day in court. Time ticked by with no resolution but plenty of phone calls with the solicitors from the DPP. There were also more interviews with the gardaí.

Some of this was just basic stuff, sorting out dates, but, at other times, I felt as if I was being tested to see if I was telling the truth. That really annoyed me at the time, though when I look at what some others have to go through in, say – rape cases – I know I got off lightly. But back then I was in my world, angry, buzzing and confused, especially confused.

I'm not sure if that is the right description. Things were starting to go a bit mad in my life. I was always a social drinker but now I was drinking heavily. Instead of taking three or four pints on a night out, I was drinking seven, eight, nine pints. Martina would try and talk to me about what was going on in my head, but my default position was to head out the door to the pub.

There were nightmares. The abuse would be replayed, down to the last bloody detail. All the time I was thinking, how did I let this happen to myself? There is no doubt that I had mostly buried the memories of Smyth, but this was bringing it all right back, night after night.

Martina, who must have been going mad herself because I wasn't allowing her to talk through what I was thinking, would try to comfort me when I woke up at night, crying. But no go. No talking for me.

At this stage, our intimacy was under pressure. Until Smyth resurfaced in our life, we had a normal, healthy, fun relationship. But the memories of the abuse triggered something in me, not a doubt about my orientation, but something more awful than that – a sense of sex being dirty, that I was dirty and somehow any physical relationship I might have with Martina was dirty, that I was abusing her. I had an overwhelming sense of guilt, and a fear that any sexual touching with Martina was the same as me abusing her. Sexual feelings were becoming tied up with what Smyth had done to me. Our sex life stopped.

Martina was patient and understanding, thank God. Later I had sessions with a counsellor and then with a psychiatrist, which helped me make sense of what was happening to me. Fundamentally I was blaming myself. But back then I hadn't a clue what was going on.

* * *

After he finished serving his sentences in Northern Ireland, Smyth was finally extradited back across the border to the Dublin authorities in March 1997. His years of abusing children had left him with an odyssey of jails, court rooms and guilty pleas. The seventy-year-old pleaded guilty quickly, to a total of 74 charges against 20 children, boys and girls, including me. The offences were committed across seven different counties and, think about this one, included charges as recent as 1993.

This really played with my head then, and still does. I had failed to stop Smyth. I had the chance to stop him but didn't, and so he carried on abusing. It was a simple equation: if I had actually stopped him in April 1975, no one would have been abused after that date.

I know now that I was drinking to cover up my feelings, drinking to hide, drinking to try and avoid feeling guilty about why I hadn't done something more back then. Did I feel responsible? Yes, of course I did. Remember too that I was back in the world of the dirty secret. No one at my work, except one man, Mick Griffin, knew anything about the court case. And at home only the closest family knew. And that's the way I wanted it to stay.

The start of the court case proper was in July that year. Because Smyth had already pleaded guilty the court hearing was really about sentencing. As it was summer I was able to combine attending the court with holidays in Ireland. We just packed up the car and away we went on the ferry with the two boys. They were fast asleep as we got closer to Holyhead, and Martina and I had a long conversation about what was ahead.

She was encouraging me to think about where I was at now. She was emphasising the fact that I had some element of control for the first time. She asked me directly how I would feel when I had to face Smyth in court, when I would see him for the first time since he had gestured at me through the window of the butcher's shop all those years ago.

I was steeling myself for that moment. There was no way he was going to get away with it. I wanted to look at him and remind him of what he had done when I was that little boy. There was talk with the DPP about me actually speaking in court, which I didn't want to do. But I definitely had to go to court and look him in the eye.

The big surprise for me when I landed in Dundalk, fresh from the boat, was the attitude of my mother and father. Both of them wanted to go to the court. I hadn't factored that in at all; I'd expected they would consider it too much. So when my father said he wanted to go, I told him there was no need, but he insisted. To me, clearly he was still upset at what he believed he had allowed to happen to his son. He was struggling with his own guilt. I wasn't going to have an argument and stop him going. If he wanted to know the details about what had happened me, he would know.

My mother said she was attending too. She was very strong in front of me, but I don't know what it was like when she went into her bedroom at night and the door was closed; she was probably in bits.

* * *

There wasn't an awful lot of chat in the car as Martina, myself and my parents drove down to the court in Dublin for that first day. There was simply a sense of determination. Each of us had been affected in different ways by Smyth and we were desperate to see some justice done.

I spotted him immediately. I couldn't miss him as he was led from a room below into the dock. Still, you had to look carefully to see the man that I remembered from 1975. In my mind's eye I had an image of a very normal-looking, kind-looking man in his early forties. The sort of man you'd think wouldn't harm a fly.

Now he was plain ugly. His shoulders were hunched. He had an outsized head, but it was his strangely shaped nose that dominated his face. His mouth seemed tied closed in a permanent grimace, or smirk, depending on what you wanted to see. As he stared out, he showed no emotion. He looked blankly ahead and did not appear to pay particular attention to what was going on around him, just glancing around occasionally.

Sitting in a gallery above the main court floor, we had a panoramic perspective of him. He was right beneath us, flanked by two guards. I remember my father saying to me that he had never felt such strength of feeling being directed at anyone as he felt during those court proceedings. 'Pure hatred,' he said. I'm not sure if I was full of hate, but I was certainly very angry with him and got angrier by the day.

Not all of the twenty people that Smyth was accused of abusing were in court but most of us were. Twelve of us. To keep our names out of it, we were all given false names; mine was 'Billy'.

The detective garda who was in charge of the case read out statements of the victims. We had the choice of speaking ourselves if we wanted. I didn't.

It was a harrowing time, all of us listening intently as the details of Smyth's offences were spelt out. What had happened to me was like a template for what happened to others. We were all abused in pretty much the same way in pretty much the same places: the car, the school, the bedroom, on trips. He was also fond of a boathouse on the shores of a County Cavan lake, and various rooms in Kilnacrott Abbey itself.

If circumstances had been different, I think I might have found the others' accounts therapeutic. It was a relief to hear that I was no different from the others who had been affected in the same way as I had. In fact, some were scarred much worse than me.

One woman's statement told how, after Smyth had left semen stains on her uniform, she was called up in front of the class by a nun and told off for having a dirty uniform. Later, when she was told that Smyth wanted to see her again, she wouldn't go, but the Reverend Mother told her she was 'above her station', and she was forced to see him.

One man explained how Smyth told him: 'God wants you to do something for me.' God apparently wanted the then twelve-year-old to masturbate Smyth. And when he didn't do it to Smyth's satisfaction the boy was told: 'God will not like you if you don't do it right.'

He faced Smyth from the witness stand and said: 'I hate him, I want to kill him. I hate priests, I just hate them. If I see one on the street, I want to go over and slap them.'

* * *

I was outside during breaks, having a cigarette, talking to some of the others and their families, when it finally struck home how so little had been done by the Church after the 1975 inquiry. And how ridiculous I was to have thought my intervention would have changed anything.

I started talking to a Belfast family and I realised they were related to the boy who had been abused with me in Dublin, who I have called 'Belfast Boy'.

I asked where he was, because it emerged he was one of the twenty victims involved in the case. I was told that Belfast Boy wasn't in the mood to talk to anyone.

It turns out that Belfast Boy, his sister and four first cousins had been abused by Smyth, the youngest of them right up to 1988. His first cousins were the victims that actually brought an end to it all because it was them who went to the police in Northern Ireland and started the first proper case against him.

I was taking all this in, thinking hard back to 1975. I couldn't make sense of what they were telling me. At that time, I had no memory of giving names and addresses to the canonical inquiry, but I knew I had told them about the trips and the abuse that had happened (the extra detail that I had given was lost to me until years later, when I saw the transcripts).

I became animated, cursing and swearing, and told the Belfast family about the inquiry I had taken part in, back in 1975. I could see that they didn't believe me at first.

Belfast Boy's uncle said to me, 'You mean you have actually taken this to the authorities, the Church people, before?' He was gobsmacked and couldn't believe what he was hearing. 'No! No, you didn't.' This man was a real committed Catholic who had already had a lot of his belief tested; now here was me telling him that the Church knew all about Brendan Smyth more than twenty years earlier.

A daughter of his, Belfast boy's first cousin, did speak to the court. She faced Smyth down: 'All through my life I have feared that man – until today. I do not fear him anymore. Today is the beginning of my life.'

She was amazingly brave, just like the others. We heard about how marriages had ended, how some had considered or even attempted suicide and how others had been left unable to form relationships. It was one heart-wrenching story after another.

After weeks of saying, 'No, I don't want to speak', I called one of the DPP's staff over and had a quick word with her. I wasn't going to leave these people on their own. I changed my mind; I would speak up.

First, my statement was read out, then it was my turn to explain the damage done. I told the court how I thought I had deprived my children.

'I cannot even hold them,' I explained. 'I love them and I want to hold them but I can't, I just can't do it.' I told how I wouldn't let the children out of my sight for fear of what might happen to them.

'I have no respect for any clergy. I tar them all with the same brush now,' I said.

The most difficult part was outlining how the abuse had seeped into my head when it came to my sexuality. 'As I grew up through my teenage years I did not know whether it was a man or a woman I wanted. I did not know what way I was sexually biased. I was never any good with girls but thankfully I developed.'

Finally, I apologised to those who had been abused after me. I thought I had done enough – I hadn't.

Afterwards, for a short time at least, I was delighted with myself. What I didn't know was that my father had fled the courtroom when the details of my abuse were being read out. I had seen him leave but assumed it was just a toilet break. The truth was he couldn't bear to hear it.

Martina told me what had happened. Just as the proceedings came around to my account, he made an awful sound, like a howling noise, and just upped and ran out. He was found outside on a bench, crying his eyes out. Someone had followed him out, a member of a support group, I think, and came across him doubled up and weeping uncontrollably.

He's told me since that he just couldn't handle what had happened to me, couldn't bear to listen to the facts of the abuse. It must have weighed on him, thinking that he had been fooled by Smyth and let me down. But as the different victims made clear, this was a familiar experience for parents and families. Smyth had made a profession of abuse but also of deceit.

* * *

There was an apology. Smyth read it out:

'I recognise all these cases for what they are – sins against God, offences against individuals and the laws of the state.'

He spoke of his 'deep sorrow and regret for any hurt or trauma these young people may have experienced'.

But no one was going to be fooled this time. Not us, the victims, and not Judge Cyril Kelly either.

The sentencing came on the third day. We made a crucial pit stop that morning on the way out of Dundalk. I went into Johnny Kirk's garage in Dundalk, on the Dublin Road, and I bought some sweets: Fruit Salads, Black Jacks and Pix 'n' Mix. I stuffed them in my coat and jumped back in the car, saying nothing to anyone about them. I had a plan.

Judge Kelly showed he had missed nothing. He took all our experiences into consideration and all that was known about Smyth. We learned that when Smyth was being transported to and from court appearances in Northern Ireland he had seen school children out playing and was sexually excited. His predatory urges couldn't be contained.

There was little in the judge's summing up that we, as victims, didn't recognise.

Smyth, he said, presented himself as 'family friend, pastor, friendly uncle, the Pied Piper, who would arrive in a car with a boot full of sweets, akin to a mobile sweetshop. That kindly man became the bogeyman.

'The psychological problems are so deep-rooted as to defy the efforts of psychotherapists. Traditional goals of management and cure are very rarely achieved and research indicates a high rate of recidivism.'

He said that, despite his age, he considered Smyth to be a continued risk to the community. At the close, Judge Kelly sentenced him to twelve years. We were thrilled.

I looked at Smyth then. He had sat throughout without giving any indication that what was going on around him really mattered. It was something to be endured. Remember that letter he wrote to Cardinal Daly? That's where you get the real Smyth, a victim who was now being sacrificed on the altar of the media and our 'exaggerated' testimony for the good of the Church.

I saw that strange nose of his beginning to twitch as the sentence was passed. I can't ever forget that nose. Even today, I can be out in a restaurant or in a pub and if I see someone with a similar nose that's me out of there. Can't abide the sight of it.

The time came for him to leave the court and so the moment had arrived for my grand plan. I reached into my pockets and pulled out the sweets. We were checked each day going into court to make sure we had no weapons on us, but I knew they wouldn't be checking for the sweets.

I passed them along, handfuls of them, to some of the other victims, to anyone who would take them, and then, just as he was being taken down into the cells below, I let rip. I hurled them at him, peppering him with the sweets.

And then from nowhere, from absolutely nowhere, came a slew of words in a voice I didn't recognise, 'Rot in hell, Smyth!'

Oh, it was me all right, but it didn't even sound like my voice, not even to me. It was some deep-rooted anger in me, that's for sure. If you want to know what it sounded like, think *The Exorcist*.

My father says now he was proud of me that day, but I am sure that I shocked him. I had shocked myself.

He and my mother had stuck by me despite their own very strong Catholic faith. I remember one time when we were outside the court and another victim, a woman who we had come to know, came up to us in tears. She said, 'Brendan, you are very lucky. Your parents believe you. My parents think I am lying. They believe the Church can do no wrong.'

Chapter 10
Legal Cases, Human Costs

The case didn't end for me there. My first enquiries about suing the Church had ended in a rebuff, maybe a rebuke, from a Dundalk solicitor a few years earlier, but I was determined to follow through now with a civil suit against the Church authorities. Most of the others were taking cases too.

I was holidaying in Galway when I was introduced to a local solicitor, Paul Horan. After that first experience in Dundalk, I had it in my head that Irish solicitors wouldn't fight the Church, so I said straight to him, 'I'm looking for a solicitor who is not afraid to tackle the Church and who will stand up against them.'

Paul said, 'I will tell you what we'll do. We will go out tomorrow and we will go to Inchagoill Island. We will sit and have a chat and you can tell me all about it, and we will take it from there.'

And that's what we did. We spent the day on this beautiful, tiny, uninhabited island on Lough Corrib and Paul was my solicitor at the day's end. He told me that it would take time and not to expect anything soon, but I can tell you neither of us expected it would take fourteen years to run its full course.

The main reason for that, I have always thought, was the legal complication with having Cardinal Sean Brady as a co-defendant. His involvement in the canonical inquiry back in 1975 didn't come out in the court. Maybe that was my fault for not remembering, or maybe no one was in a hurry to put his name into the ring.

It took another journalist, a *Sunday Mirror* reporter called Declan White, to put Cardinal Brady's name in the spotlight. White followed up the scant detail about the secret inquiry given in court and discovered the identity of the mysterious third priest – Fr John B. Brady.

The *Sunday Mirror* (10 August 1997) quoted a Church spokesman as saying:

'Father Seán Brady, now Archbishop of Armagh, was at the time of the 1975 tribunal a fulltime post-primary teacher and a part-time secretary to the diocese of Kilmore. He was asked by the Bishop of Kilmore to attend the tribunal in Dundalk. Father Brady's role was to record the boy's evidence.'

There was no mention of what I had told the secret Church inquiry, no mention of all those names I had given, no mention of what the Church had done with the information and, of course, no mention of the second secret interview with Cavan Boy.

It seems extraordinary now but the story appeared to die there. Because he was representing me, Paul Horan spotted it, but most in the Irish media ignored it. And Cardinal Brady's role wasn't scrutinised further. However, the issue did not go away.

Roll on another ten days or so to the 21 August. The first legal letters were sent to the Church and the Norbertine Order by my solicitor. Twenty-four hours later – a bombshell.

We were back home in England when the phone rang. It was my father.

'Crack open the champagne – Smyth is dead.'

Smyth had dropped dead of a heart attack on the 22 August, less than a month into his jail term at the Curragh prison. I knew what my father meant, but I couldn't celebrate. I put the phone down and turned to Martina and said, 'He's got away with it again. Now the victims do his sentence.'

* * *

I have always thought that Smyth got away easy in the end, but I have come to understand that, while he was personally responsible for causing so much hurt, there are other culprits in this story. The cover-up is the issue. And that goes all the way back to the 1950s, then the 1960s, the 1970s and the 1980s. The Church knew about Fr Brendan Smyth. The Norbertine Order and the local Kilmore diocese. Even the former Papal Nuncio, Gaetano Alibrandi, if Fr Bruno Mulvihill is correct.

I was like a haunted man in the days after his death. My father had called it wrong this once. Smyth had been a reliable target, if you like; I could point to him, and shout at him as I did in court that day. He was my bogeyman. His death complicated things and deepened my frustration. As long as he was alive I could take satisfaction that he was paying for his deeds; in death there was no satisfaction at all. The previous three years, in particular, and my childhood had been so shaped by him. I think he had become a permanent fixture in my life. With him jailed and my role in his jailing, I had managed to get some control. Now that control was gone, but his mark, his impact, remained.

If I had been sufficiently together at the time, I might have headed back to Ireland for the funeral, just to see him head off to wherever he was going. Hell, if there is such a place, I think.

It was a very unusual funeral by all accounts. Firstly it happened in the dead of night. Mass was said at the chapel in the Holy Trinity Abbey sometime before half past four in the morning. It was still dark when Smyth's coffin was taken to the cemetery in the Abbey grounds and he was interred. Lights from a hearse were used to light up the graveside as the coffin was lowered. No more than twelve people attended the service, most of them Norbertine priests. Three or four members of the gardaí were there too, presumably to keep members of the public, or journalists, away. The Press arrived too late to witness the ceremony. The grave was eventually covered in concrete to stop it being vandalised.

* * *

You would think it would be easy to figure out where you stand about the Catholic Church if you'd been through what I have. Well it's not, at least not for anyone in my family. Some of the victims declared their hatred for the Church; me, I declared my loss of respect for priests. There's a difference. Priests, nuns, the Church itself had been part of my life, like most Irish Catholics, from the point of birth.

All the significant milestones in my life were over-seen by priests: Baptism, Holy Communion, primary school, Confirmation, secondary school, marriage. And that's just me. The same went for all in my family. Is it any wonder that I found it difficult to reach a final definitive conclusion about the Church? It was part of me. And the point I'm making is that it was also part of everyone I knew to a greater or lesser degree. My mother and father, for example.

This goes to explain some extraordinary paperwork, mostly correspondence, that involves my parents and the Church. There is also a letter written by Martina that I knew nothing about until relatively recently. All the paperwork came to light during the later legal proceedings.

It seems that shortly after the sentencing of Smyth my father wrote to Cardinal Brady. We knew that the prelate had taken part in the inquiry, but my father had no idea what had actually happened, what questions had been put or even the vow of secrecy that I had to take. He and my mother had seen a counsellor, who had advised that they put their thoughts down on paper and write to the Church.

It says much that they were so upset that they went to get counselling. So much had impacted on them and their children from that first apparently innocent visit by Smyth all those years ago. My father has said since that he and my mother were in desperate need of someone to help them make sense of what was going on. They needed to talk it all through with an independent voice.

I am not sure what my father wrote in that first letter. I think he wondered why the Church hadn't made a proper apology for what Smyth had done, and been allowed to do. But I do know what happened as a consequence of it.

On Thursday, 25 September 1997, Cardinal Brady (then still the Archbishop of Armagh) left word with priests at the Redeemer parochial house that he wanted to arrange a visit to my mother and father that very evening. Fr Eamonn McCamley organised matters for the Archbishop. He landed down about five o'clock and told my parents that the Archbishop would be arriving within the hour.

Fr McCamley later wrote a detailed note of what happened that evening and sent it on to Archbishop Brady. It was accompanied by a one-page letter, where Fr McCamley says he would be pleased to make any necessary corrections, should 'Your Grace' feel some changes should be made or if anything had been omitted.

In the note Fr McCamley explains how: 'The Archbishop was warmly welcomed and Mr Boland said how thankful he and his wife were that the Archbishop took the time to visit and that there was no need. Frank (my father) also said that the Archbishop's visit meant so much to him.'

The note continues: 'The Archbishop expressed that he wanted to visit them and tell them how sorry he was on his own behalf, and also as Archbishop and their parish priest. This was very well received.'

My father did most of the talking during the half-hour meeting, according to the note. He explained how the Smyth affair had caused so much damage to me, and the family generally. He also told how it was me who had shouted out 'Rot in Hell'.

Fr McCamley wrote: 'Archbishop Brady listened to their story and offered his sincerest apology.'

What exactly was Archbishop Brady apologising for? In my opinion, he wasn't apologising for anything *he* did or didn't do. It seemed to me to be a generic apology, one of those apologies you hear people in public life make all the time, a version of 'I am sorry for your troubles'.

Days later, my father wrote again to Archbishop Brady. The opening lines say it all: 'I wish to thank you most sincerely for your visit to my house ... My wife and I were honoured by the fact that we were speaking to you, Your Grace, just like a friend and we were overawed by your humility.'

The letter ends: 'May our Blessed Lady, through the intercession of my favourite saint, Naomh Brid, watch over you and our country.'

Archbishop Brady also wrote about the meeting and my parents: 'They are good humble people – hurt by events.'

He then noted: 'No mention was made of the assurances. They did refer to my promising to pray for them ...'

His note reflects the tone of the visit and it is sympathetic as far as my family goes, but the fact that he chose to record that my father didn't raise 'the assurances' leads me to suspect that he considered this of some importance.

Those 'assurances' appear to be a reference to what my father and I recalled was said after the 1975 canonical inquiry, when we were assured that Smyth would be dealt with and that he wouldn't be able to abuse children again. These assurances would feature prominently in my civil case.

Back then, as far as my father and mother were concerned, Archbishop Brady had brought the Holy

Spirit into their home. At this point, there was no thought of legal action on their part; instead, they were genuinely honoured that he chose to visit them and listen to what they had to say. After what they had been through, this was almost vindication for their faith in the Church.

There would be more letters from my father, but the tone would shift, and shift radically.

Martina and I were in counselling ourselves four months later when she wrote her own letter and sent it to Cardinal Brady and to Monsignor Francis Donnelly, the Dundalk-based priest who told investigating gardaí that he was the note-taker at the inquiry. She didn't show me the letter at the time, just wrote it up and posted it, along with a poem she had written for me. Typical of her, it went straight to the point from the very first line.

I am writing this letter to you in desperation. I am the wife of one of Fr. Brendan Smyth's victims. At this particular moment in my family life, my husband and myself are finding it very hard to cope. Our lives have been turned upside down by this whole process of the Catholic Church ...

Brendan was abused by Smyth some 27 years ago
… you yourselves met him when he was a scared
twelve-year-old [sic], you both questioned him …
but never to this day has he ever known the outcome
of that meeting. He dreams about you questioning
him (and he does not even know you) but even in
his dreams and nightmares he gets no answers.

… At the moment my husband is reliving his
life through the eyes of his own 2 sons who are
twelve and nine years old. As they are getting older
daily life gets harder. Would you be afraid for your
nieces or nephews to attend mass? School? Parties?
Or anywhere for that matter for fear of who will
talk to them, get to know them, get into their
minds and abuse them.

I myself went to our own Parish Priest …
to explain our cry for help, but his answer was
Brendan must forgive and forget.

… In my heart of hearts you and Monsignor
Francis Donnelly who were present at the Meeting
held the key in your hands that night to put an end
to Smyth, and you both did nothing. You hid that
key like so many other times to follow and let him
continue to carry on, and carry on, and carry on.
But last July at the court case Brendan apologised

to all those who were abused after him on your behalves, and I was proud of him. Yes, you yourselves have also contributed to Brendan's state of mind, he was used again.

... How can I explain to a 37-year-old man that he did not ask for the abuse to happen? How can I explain to our children the different Dad they are now living with? How can I explain to our friends that we do not want to socialise with them? What reasons do I give to my children when their dad says he does not want to live anymore? Are you going to give me answers on how to cope or are you just going to tell me that you will pray for us? Time will heal.

I wonder have you both ever in 27 years considered – thought – understood – or felt the hurt and destruction that this man has caused, to us as a family and as Catholics, because believe me you would not be able to carry out your daily duties.

Accompanying the letter was a poem Martina had written for me, as a 'small piece of consolation'. Unlike the letter, I did see this when it was written. Then, even though I was still in the middle of battling with all the demons that had been set free in my head, I felt that I had made a very lucky choice in my life's partner. It is a poem all about love.

> *I feel your feelings,*
> *I feel your pain,*
> *I feel I have let you down, by not*
> *being part of what happened to you.*
>
> *We have gone through everything*
> *in our lives together from our*
> *teenage years – but this one thing.*
>
> *I want to help, and don't know how.*
> *I will not let him hurt you*
> *anymore.*
> *I will not let him break us.*
> *You have me and the boys.*
> *Something he will never share.*
> *We love you.*
> *Martina & the Boys.*

I don't know if Martina's poem and the letter had any impact on Archbishop Brady and Monsignor Francis Donnelly because they never responded to her.

* * *

Martina has always said that I was a changed man after 1994 when the news broke about Smyth. And not for the better. But she'll also tell you that I was a different man again after the court case and Smyth's death – that when we travelled over for the court case she thought there was the old Brendan returning, but, in fact, by the time that summer was ended I was in worse shape than ever.

I know I was drinking very heavily and I know our sex life had essentially ended. The counselling sessions had started, which helped to a degree, but I still couldn't get things focused again. The counselling sessions were really about marital relations. Martina got something from them. I didn't because I don't think they addressed the issues I was dealing with: the abuse, my guilt and my general frustrations.

There were nights I would roll in at four or five in the morning after a snooker and pints night. I'm sure it was testing every bit of Martina's patience and love. Her continued devotion was the difference between me heading off the deep end mentally – maybe killing myself or just drinking myself to death – and me holding on to my sanity.

* * *

My father was keeping an eye on me through all this. He did know about Martina's letter and he knew it hadn't been answered. You cannot imagine a more peaceable, affable man, a man who I have only ever seen angry maybe two or three times. But the letters he started to dispatch to Cardinal Brady were a study in barely restrained anger. There was grief in them too.

The letters, I have seen three of them, all talk about how the family's Catholic faith was damaged. I'll quote from just one. Written about 2000, it begins by saying that, despite the strong Catholic faith of my father and mother, all the children had fallen out with the Church, and now only go to mass when it suits them. My father also wrote about his fears that this would affect the faith of his grandchildren.

He writes: 'You can imagine the emotional pain that this causes. It leaves in its wake a kind of pain that's never resolved.'

We were close but we didn't talk about emotions. I would tell him how I was doing and then he would have to figure out the rest for himself. But these letters are full of his truth.

Imagine you are him, writing this as you head into your 80th year, and you are watching one of the pillars of your life disintegrate in front of you. The

Catholic faith had provided the basis for how he lived his life and how he expected us to live ours. He was in bits. I didn't see that then; I was too full of my own dramas.

In the very next line in the letter he states: 'I would like you to know that my family is my reason for living – they are all fine upstanding citizens of the highest character and integrity.'

My father was making clear that his priority was his family, not the Church, despite all he believed in.

He then tells Archbishop Brady that he knows that Martina's letter received no reply from him and Monsignor Donnelly. He adds: 'Let me educate you, Your Excellency, the word "SORRY" would have meant a lot at that time!'

He goes on to remind Archbishop Brady about the visit he made in to the family in 1997:

'... at the time the most I expected was a letter or a phone call from you. But to my great surprise my wife and I were graced with a personal visit from you ... and we were truly honoured by that most generous gesture.

'What I can't understand is why you never wrote back to apologise to Brendan and his wife. After all it was him that was abused. I have come to the conclusion that it all came down to the "FILTHY LUCRE" – or in other words … compensation.'

I am amazed at his tone in those letters. For such a staunch Catholic, to speak to the head of the Church like that was pretty amazing. He was putting up a big fight, his own fight. I now know that he and Martina were talking about me, trying to help find a way forward for me. His letter writing was his way of pitching in.

Archbishop Brady did write to my father to say that 'his failure to reply to Martina is connected to the fact the Church is being sued and that I have been named as a defendant in the case.'

And I know that in Cardinal Brady's final letter to my father, or at least the last one that is on record, he wrote: 'I am deeply sorry for what has happened to Brendan. I pray for all of you often.'

I think that you can see the guiding hands of lawyers behind all of this. One priest, who I know sits close to the power base in the Irish Catholic Church, told a friend that often the hands of the individual churchmen and women were tied by legal advice to admit nothing. The priest said the churchmen may want to respond in a more open, human way but dared not because of the potential legal liability. In other words, if they admitted fault with a proper apology then the flood gates might open. In effect, their ability to give a fuller apology, as they may have wished to, was constrained by legal proceedings. That is the legal situation; but are churchmen not supposed to be God's ambassadors, God's representatives on earth?

The money never mattered to me. What I wanted was an admission and an apology. For that I would have to wait.

* * *

The Norbertine Order, which had the normal day-to-day authority over Smyth, was destined to take the responsibility for meeting the legal bills from the civil cases for his abuse. The Norbertines sold more than 160 acres of farmland in the 1990s to meet that bill. The sale raised €620,000 but that wouldn't prove to be enough because there were so many victims.

The risk of financial liability because of abusing clerics had been troubling the Irish Church for years. I first learned about this from the state inquiry into clerical abuse in the Dublin Archdiocese which resulted in the Murphy Report.

It had been commissioned by the Irish state in the wake of a series of allegations of abuse and cover-up in the Dublin archdiocese. Judge Yvonne Murphy headed the inquiry, which was tasked with investigating how the Church and State authorities handled the allegations.

It published its findings in 2009. Its conclusions were devastating, showing exactly how the Church was embroiled in a policy of cover-up. Later, four bishops would resign, although they denied any wrongdoing. However, it was the revelations about the Church and efforts to insure against the risk of paedophile priests that really intrigued me.

The Murphy Report stated:

> The evidence reviewed by the Commission suggests that serious consideration was first given in 1986 to obtaining specific insurance cover for the benefit of the Archdiocese of Dublin for any potential liability falling upon it arising out of child sexual abuse by a priest of the Archdiocese. The timing is significant because the date of seeking insurance cover is clearly a date by which the Archdiocese had developed a realisation that child sexual abuse was a serious problem for it.

The following year the archdiocese started talking to the Church and General Insurance Company about a policy. Here comes the cunning bit – on the part of the Church – Church and General seem to have been given to understand that the Dublin bishops were just playing safe after what they'd seen in America. But the insurer had been led up the garden path.

The Murphy Report also noted:

> It need hardly be pointed out by this Commission that the Archbishop's understanding of the need for insurance came from events much closer to home than the USA. At this time, the Archdiocese had knowledge of approximately 20 priests against whom allegations had been made, or about whom there were suspicions or concerns.
>
> At the time the Archdiocese took out insurance in 1987, Archbishop Kevin McNamara, Archbishop Dermot Ryan and Archbishop John Charles McQuaid had had, between them, available information on complaints against at least 17 priests operating under the aegis of the Dublin Archdiocese. The taking out of insurance was an act proving knowledge of child sexual abuse as a potential major cost to the Archdiocese and is inconsistent with the view that Archdiocesan officials were still "on a learning curve" at a much

later date, or were lacking in an appreciation of the phenomenon of clerical child sex abuse.

The first premium paid was IR£515. Within a year, all other Irish dioceses, with one exception, had signed up to similar policies. It didn't take too long before the insurance company realised what a cesspit of abuse was opening up.

The Report quotes from a Church and General document in 1995: 'a number of high profile cases are not covered by the special policy because of prior knowledge on the part of the diocese concerned.' The company cancelled the policy the following year.

So what do you make of that? Here is the Church knowing that it has up to 20 abusers (in just one diocese) and it goes to an insurance company and looks for cover for abuse. But it doesn't say why it needs the cover – it says nothing of the problem in its backyard. I wonder is that a sin? A venal sin or a mortal sin? Or is OK to behave like that as long as you are seeking to protect God's Church?

That same report tells the astonishing story of how a female contraceptive was used to treat one persistent paedophile priest. The Dublin archdiocese had sent him to America for treatment, to a specialist centre set up by a Catholic order, the Congregation of the Servants of the Paraclete. They are an interesting bunch themselves and were, and are, dedicated to helping priests who have problems, not just priests who abuse.

Dozens of Irish priests, including Smyth, were sent to their centre in England, at Stroud in Gloucestershire, as well as to the American facilities. One of the most amazing things about the Paraclete is that I think they understood the threat these abusing priests posed and were shouting about it to the Church authorities from as far back as the 1950s.

The priest who founded the order, Fr Gerald Fitzgerald, contemplated buying an island in the Caribbean, in Grenada, to house paedophile priests. This is part of what he said in a letter to an American archbishop in 1957: 'It is for this class of rattlesnake that I have always wished for an island retreat – but even an island is too good for these vipers, of whom the Gentle Master said, "It were better they had not been born."'

In the end, the growing popularity of the area for tourism ended that plan.

The Murphy Report also outlined the story of one of the most notorious paedophile priests from the Dublin archdiocese, Fr Patrick McCabe. In 1983, after repeated and failed efforts to control his abusive tendencies, he was sent to a Paraclete treatment centre in New Mexico, where he was dosed with the female contraceptive drug Depo-Provera. This was apparently supposed to work by knocking back his testosterone levels to pretty much zero and thus killing his libido.

Reports came back to the Dublin archdiocese saying it was effective, but now the Church had a problem: how to source a female contraceptive in a state where it was banned – in large part because of their opposition to it.

So there you have it. The Catholic women of Ireland were forbidden to use contraceptives, but it was fine for a paedophile priest. As it turned out, Fr McCabe stopped taking the drug and started to abuse again, in the US and then in Ireland too.

A couple of years after this chemical intervention the Dublin bishops signed up to a special insurance policy without a whisper about their problem clerics.

All of this was done in secret. And it only came out into the open when the Church began to cooperate with the authorities. Just like the details about the canonical inquiry, which were also kept secret. It was one thing admitting that Cardinal Brady (Fr John B. Brady as he was then) had taken notes at an inquiry involving one young boy, it was quite another to reveal the full story of all that happened around the inquiry, and ultimately, all that didn't happen.

* * *

The opening letters in my civil legal case had been sent in August 1997. My solicitor, Paul Horan, had written to the Norbertine Order and the Church authorities, threatening to sue because they had known that Fr Brendan Smyth was abusing children but they had failed to act.

The very first letter was sent on 21 August. It laid out the grounds for the case which ultimately hit the headlines.

Paul wrote:

We are instructed that an Ecclesiastical Court/ Tribunal was held in Dundalk in or about the year 1975 where, inter alia, our client's case was heard and an apology was tendered to our client and his parents and an undertaking given that Fr Smyth would not be allowed to sexually abuse children again.

Our client was completely devastated therefore to learn that notwithstanding the said undertaking given, Fr Smyth was permitted subsequent to the said Ecclesiastical Court/Tribunal to come in contact with and sexually abuse children again. The great guilt, anxiety and upset that this has caused our client is a matter of grave concern.

Paul also requested all records of the canonical inquiry.

Please furthermore note that we also call on you to furnish voluntary Discovery on Oath of all the proceedings of the Ecclesiastical Court/Tribunal, including all submissions, reports, letters, notes, findings, recordings, decisions, transcripts and judgements thereof.

He requested that this documentation be delivered in thirty-five days. It would be thirteen *years* before the Church released those documents. By then the court proceedings had changed and taken on a new twist or two.

More significantly, my own life and that of my family had changed forever.

Chapter 11
What to Tell the Children

I didn't tell my children, Niall and Stephen, about Smyth and the abuse and the canonical inquiry until I thought the time was right. They were growing up oblivious to it all except for what they must have thought was the very strange ban I had on them doing anything that Martina and I couldn't supervise.

I was to learn soon enough that bad things have a way of happening anyway. You can take all the precautions and then life just does its thing, or as I thought for a long time, *God* does his thing.

On occasion, I did allow them to have their friends overnight but not often, and I didn't let them go to others' houses for sleepovers. Any time Stephen or Niall challenged me about our policy of supervising them I just killed the discussion stone dead. Like when Stephen had asked about why I wouldn't let him join the altar boys.

The two lads were coming along nicely, regardless. We didn't put them forward for Confirmation. I wasn't going to force them deeper into a religion that I didn't really have much faith in, so I was leaving it to them, when they were old enough, if they wanted to be confirmed as a Catholic. After 1997 we had stopped going to mass and didn't see why we should push our children into the Church when we didn't go regularly ourselves. We still went at Christmas and Easter.

Christmas was important to us. We'd pack up the car and head back to Ireland, to visit my family and Martina's too. There were times you felt you were on a merry-go-round with all the homes you were obliged to call to, not that I am complaining.

The car was normally stuffed with presents for the boys. The trick, as every parent knows, is to parcel them up when the kids are asleep. Because we were travelling on the boat we had to pack up a day or two early. One Christmas morning Stephen came rushing into the bedroom cheering, 'Yes! I knew if I prayed hard enough, I would get the stuff I saw in the boot of the car.' You have to laugh.

The Irish cousins were always teasing our two boys because of their English accents. But I knew the boys really enjoyed the Irish Christmas. After the dinner, the children were put to work in nativity plays. There were card games, bingo and lots of singing. Great nights.

Football was still the boys' number one interest (they must have got their talent from Martina because they didn't get it from me). For us, the only problem was that they played at different age levels. Because of our supervision rule, I would go and watch one game and Martina the other. Always, we were with them.

Stephen was on Charlton's Young Boys' books and Niall was on Ipswich's Young Boys' books, so we had quite a bit of travelling to do. Martina normally took Niall and I would take Stephen. And if they weren't playing at the same time, Stephen would come with us to Niall's matches and Niall would come with us to Stephen's.

Niall played in a sweeping position, though he was really a midfielder who ended up falling back into the sweeper's role. He did really, really well. Stephen was a right-back and very good at it. Both of them played with Essex county teams.

* * *

We were very close, the four of us, even as Stephen moved into his teenage phase. He was once described as a loveable rogue, which certainly captures part of him. He loved fun and was outgoing, and could get into the odd scrape. Niall was more reserved.

Stephen had his own ways of doing things. It didn't matter who had a different opinion; it always had to be done Stephen's way. And I am not just talking about home, I am talking about at school. If the teacher had an idea, but Stephen wanted to do it one way, he would have to do it his way. He was a bright boy, very bright. And very funny. He knew I wasn't a great fan of Manchester United, but he went out one day and bought a United shirt and put it on, just to have a go at me. A great wind up. Brilliant, especially considering he was a Chelsea fan.

The most trouble he ever got into was a fight on the way home from school. It was his last year in school and he was accused of hitting someone while wearing his school uniform. There were two of them in it, but the other lad got to tell his side of the story first. Stephen was suspended.

I had a go at Stephen. He explained to me that it wasn't really a fight. There was no blood drawn, nothing. Something silly over a girl, I think. I went down to the school and tried to argue Stephen's case. They said he was in school uniform and he was still representing the school until he got home and got out of his uniform.

Then comes word that the Board of Governors had met and decided to expel him. This was an important year because it was coming up to his exams and, though the teachers there used to send him homework, he was in danger of really making a mess of things.

We called a meeting with the school. I had written down all these things I was going to say to the governors. I was so nervous and when I started explaining why they should let Stephen back in I started spluttering and lost the run of my thoughts immediately.

Then Stephen stepped up. He says, 'First of all I would like to say that I apologise for fighting with that kid. It was a silly fight with nothing personal in it.'

And on he went. Totally fluent for half an hour. He was fantastic. I remember wondering where all that confidence came from 'cause he certainly didn't get it from me. A day or so later, a letter from the board of governors arrived – he was back in.

*　*　*

He did well enough in the end and then he got an apprenticeship at News International, where I worked. I asked one of the interview panel, because there were a lot of others in for it, if he had got the job on his own merits. I was told, yes.

He was just seventeen. Most of his time was spent away in college, studying, up and down to Stratford College in London every day.

After he started, he came home and told me that he'd been asked to join the job pension scheme. He said he didn't think it would be worth it because he would get docked £26 pounds a month from his wages. And for him that was a lot. First year apprentice wages were not great, just over £12,000 a year. I advised him to join, but he seemed set on not joining so we left it like that.

That Christmas was special. We celebrated it at home in England, which was a rarity. And another thing we did that year – we allowed Stephen and Niall to open their presents on Christmas Eve, or open some of them at least. Later, when we were all sitting around watching the old black and white Christmas films, I decided to tell the boys about Smyth and everything.

I went to the attic and took down all the old newspaper clippings I had about the case. I think I tried to explain to them: 'This is why you didn't go on your school trips. And why you didn't get to be an altar boy.'

They took it all in and I don't think they even asked one question. But it was very important for me to have explained finally why we had those rules. I wanted things to make sense for them.

It turns out the timing was very significant.

* * *

Me and the boys had organised a surprise fortieth birthday present for Martina – a trip to the Maldives, to one of those perfect holiday resorts you only dream about. She had had a tough couple of years, not just coping with me but with a series of back problems, major operations and finally a diagnosis of multiple sclerosis the previous summer. It has never progressed thankfully; neither has it gone away.

The night we surprised her she thought she was going on a regular family outing to the Pak Lok Chinese restaurant with me, Niall and Stephen and his girlfriend, Claire.

Wing, the owner of the restaurant, helped our little conspiracy. He hid the plane tickets in a menu, along with £100 the boys had saved. When Martina discovered the tickets, she cried and we all hugged. We left for the Maldives two days later.

Stephen was going to stay in the house, and Niall, still only fourteen, was going to stay with our close friends, Gill and Tony Tohill.

Before we left, the last thing I said to Stephen was 'Make sure you go to work. Go to college every day. Don't let me down.' And he just looked at me like – well – of course he was going to do all of this.

So off to the Maldives. For our first ever holiday on our own since the children were born. When we got there, it was just like paradise. We had to take a boat out to our resort on the island of Meeru. This place was truly fabulous. Everywhere was sand. The bars and the restaurants were sand-floored. Just an amazing place. We were in a beach hut and you would wake up in the morning and the sea was in front of you. Just paradise.

We did a walk of the island every night. The whole island. Forty-five minutes it took. We were having a great time. Met a few other couples. Cooking on the beach. Night-time fishing. This was heaven.

I had organised dinner on the beach, with candles and fine wines, for Martina's actual birthday on 30 January. They used shells to write out on the table 'Happy Birthday Martina'.

So you have it – we are having the time of our lives.

*　*　*

A few days later, on 4 February 2003, it was time to celebrate my forty-second birthday. Another magic night. We had gone back to our chalet around 1 o'clock in the morning. Martina couldn't sleep with an awful pain in her side. She was up and down most of the night, which is why she could hear a text message coming through on my phone.

She looked at it – I was now up too – and she saw it was a message from Claire, Stephen's lovely girlfriend.

Martina read it quickly, and turned to me and said, 'There is something wrong. Stephen and Claire must have had a row.'

Claire had written: 'Stephen is my best friend, my first love and I will never forget him.'

And it was just when I was reading the text that the phone rang. It was Claire. She said, 'There has been an accident.'

I went out the door with the phone and asked, 'How bad is he?'

She said, 'He is dead.'

I couldn't tell Martina. I went back in the room and I said, 'Look, there has been an accident. Pack the bag, just pack the bags. We are going home.'

I ran to the reception to try to get someone to help us find a way home. The bloke there asked me what was wrong. I explained as best I could, and then I told him that I couldn't give the news to Martina. I asked him to tell her.

He said, 'I will come with you and I will sit with you, but you will have to tell her, right. I can't tell her.' And he came down with me.

Martina was in tears when we got back, but she was still thinking that it was an accident, not the worst news ever.

I remember the guy from reception coming into the room and he sat in the corner.

He said, 'Brendan, talk to your wife.'

I had never prepared for a conversation like this. Ever. Can you imagine delivering this news? I just yelled, 'He's dead!'

Martina fired something at me, a hairbrush, something. She was utterly devastated.

I contacted the police in England and they confirmed the news. Interpol were looking for us. Apparently Claire had been told not to contact us, but we are both glad she did.

We only made two other calls. I phoned Stephen's godparents, my brother-in-law Jimmy and Martina's sister Fionnuala. I got them to tell my parents. They were in Harlow before us.

The worst of it was the trip home. Insurance papers couldn't be found. I said, just put us on whatever flights will get us home. We had to go over to the main island and we had to spend the night in a hotel there. The two of us just lay on the bed, looking at the ceiling, not talking to each other, not even a word. We were speechless with grief.

The next morning we had to fly further again – from Malé over to Sri Lanka to get a plane back to Heathrow. It took us two days to get home. We could only get tickets in first class on the way back from Sri Lanka. The stewardess kept coming around.

'Would you like wine?'

'No. No. I don't want anything.'

'Would like to look at the menu?'

'No. I want absolutely nothing.'

So then she comes over and asks, 'Why would you pay all this money, if you are not going to avail yourself of anything?'

I lost it. The time for dignity was long gone. I told her my son was killed in an accident. She must have been mortified. It was wrong of me to lose it with her, but she took in our situation, apologised and pulled the curtain. We just slept the rest of the journey.

When the plane landed at Heathrow, the doors opened and in walked two policemen. They were calling out for Mr and Mrs Ballino: 'Can Mr and Mrs Ballino please make themselves known?' Not Boland. Some

SWORN TO SILENCE

mad spelling mistake. They found us and escorted us off the plane. We were ushered straight through security. There was no such thing as passport control.

We were taken into this big room, where two of my friends, Seán Whelan and Tony Tohill, were waiting. It was pure surreal. The four of us all crying in this massive room with nothing in it but ourselves and four bottles of mineral water.

We still couldn't believe it. I kept saying, he is going to be at home when I get there. All the way back in the car we didn't speak a single word to Seán and Tony. And they couldn't talk to us because they didn't know what to say.

I do remember asking them one question: 'Is it true?'

'Yes.'

* * *

When we finally got home, Niall was standing waiting on us. I didn't say anything to him; I just hugged him. We held him. All our families were there too, having travelled already from Ireland.

I was very grateful for something Niall did after he learned that Stephen was dead. Before he went out, Stephen had taken a shower and he left bits of his clothes in the bathroom; the towel was lying on the floor somewhere else, everything askew in that messy teenager way.

Niall told anyone, who was trying to help, that he didn't want anything touched. He wanted it left exactly the way it was.

A police liaison officer met me at home. My first job was to go and identify Stephen. My father, who had already arrived ahead of us, insisted on going with me.

I was taken to Stephen. He was lying in a room with a blanket, or cover, over his body. Someone pulled it down and I asked to be alone with him for a minute.

Oh, I laid into Stephen. I called him all the names.

'You stupid fucker! Look what you have done now!'

I'd been told that he had taken the keys of my car and gone jaunting around, before the car crashed and he was killed.

I got that over with and then I just kissed him.

It was my car he crashed in. I had hidden the keys, but somehow he found them.

Initially we were told that Stephen was driving my car and he crashed the car. The car tumbled over and ended up hitting a tree. Simple as that. Since then I have learned more.

There was a race, between two cars, and one of the cars tipped the back of my car. The car flipped over, hit a tree and Stephen was killed. The worst part for me is that Stephen died alone. I have lots of unresolved questions about that night, but that is the worst of it, that no one spoke to him, or held him.

The first day we went to see Stephen in the funeral home Martina noticed his hair wasn't done, his nails were black. There was dirt under his nails. Our good friend Seán Whelan went up and he did Stephen's hair, cleaned his nails. But there was another problem. Unlike in Ireland where the funeral follows two or three days after the death, in England it can take weeks for the formalities to be done.

So we had half of Dundalk over, to stand by us, and they wanted to visit Stephen as we did. We discovered you had to make an appointment to see your son at the undertakers. One day there was a virtual standoff until the police liaison officer stepped in and explained to the undertakers how it should work. In the end, they allowed us pretty much unrestricted access for a twenty-four-hour period, which was what we wanted.

Inevitably there were all sorts of problems organising the funeral mass. We decided to ask Fr Eamonn McCamley to come over. He did a great job. He was the first priest that I actually put faith in after every other one that I had trouble with. And when he came over to do Stephen's funeral, he had a note from Cardinal Brady, saying he was sorry to hear about our son.

I took Stephen down home for the last night, to wake him before he was buried. He had an open coffin, which spooked some people who weren't used to the Irish way of doing things. Others thought it beautiful. Death means something different to different people. Some are afraid of a corpse. We sat up all night with him, the men, just like in Ireland.

The funeral was huge, one of the biggest crowds ever seen at a local funeral. Harlow was at a standstill for hours. All the florists had closed because they had all run out of flowers. I had asked Mick Griffin, the first person at work that I had confided in, if he would speak at the funeral mass. Well, what he prepared was an amazing tribute. He had the whole church in tears. Afterwards Stephen was buried in a cemetery in Harlow.

Martina wanted to bury Stephen in Ireland, but I disagreed because I knew you need somewhere to grieve; you need somewhere to go. You need to go to the graveside. In fact, we went to the grave to see him every single day, three times a day. It was like that for twelve months or so, and then we took a conscious decision to ease off, visiting him twice a week or three times a week instead.

* * *

We would never make Niall go up, but we hoped that he would make his own way up there. After Stephen died, Niall, who was quiet anyway, went totally into himself. Niall had seen Stephen and his friend going away in my car that last night. He said to me that he should have tried to stop him. He was left with issues over that and I think that's why he is so quiet and deep now.

I had another take on the events.

I decided that Stephen's death was God's punishment for me suing the Church. There was a song I knew that said it all as far as I was concerned. It was from an Irish band called Bagatelle and it was called 'Trump Card'.

For me that is a song that has been written from the Church to me. The words go:

> *I'm gonna play my trump card,*
> *and don't you know, it's gonna go hard with*
> * you, …*
> *Well you'll be sorry, well you'll be sorry when the*
> * day comes to pass,*
> *I've had enough of your dreams, I've had enough*
> * of your schemes,*
> *I'm going to show my true colours at last.*

Retribution it was, pure and simple. I was being punished for suing the Church. People said, don't be stupid, but you had to be in my shoes to actually feel it. I had failed again.

It's a crazy idea. Why would God punish someone who didn't do anything wrong? But that's what happens. He punishes the wrong people. The wrong people die. Look at the civilians in wars.

So any time I had drink on me, I would put on this music. I was eating myself up with guilt. I can see that now, but then it was just more crap being thrown at my life. My fault.

At some point, Martina had had enough and she put the CD players in the attic. That helped, but I have only lately, in the last three or four years, managed to persuade myself that I was delusional. And I am still not certain. I haven't listened to that song for a while but it will always be imprinted on my brain.

There was another Bagatelle song that could have been written just for Stephen, and it's the other side of the coin. It's called 'Second Violin'.

'*I would have given you anything that you wanted, I would have taken you anywhere you wanted to go.*'

Still love it.

I would find it difficult to listen to the type of music Stephen liked: dance, garage and house music. But one evening, not long before he died, he was upstairs studying; he was playing the song 'Feel' by Robbie Williams over and over again. I peeped in and sarcastically asked if he liked that song. He just nodded, yes. The significance of this song is the lyrics. One line says that God is laughing at my plans. Well, wasn't he just?

I asked Fr McCamley if we could play the song at the funeral mass. He listened to it and he had no objections. This song has a habit of coming on the radio at very significant times, around Stephen's birthday or his anniversary or another family event. I believe he is letting us know he is looking after us.

* * *

It took us months to get up the courage to go out again. Most of the time we were inside with my music driving everyone mad. Our friends Tony and Gill would come round every Saturday night. They'd sit with us and listen to my shit. My crying. They put up with that for over a year. Gill had been particularly affected by Stephen's death. That night of the accident she had the job of giving Niall the news. She is still suffering from that.

Meanwhile, Martina had given up her job at the nursery. She couldn't work with children any more.

Every child that came in made her think of Stephen. She did get another job, working as a carer with the elderly, not kids.

There was one bright moment, which sort of shone a way into the future. We took a break in Majorca with friends. They'd bought the tickets and practically forced us onto the plane. Once we got there, we found a real peace. We were away from the Shadow of Death. And the place we were staying in was old traditional Majorca, not all high rise and discos.

Something very strange happened on that holiday. Niall and I were playing a game of pool in a local pub. I left him playing with youngsters and went to the bar. I was standing there when this woman came up to me. She said, 'I don't wish to spook you, but I can see a young man standing beside you.'

I went 'Sorry?' and she said again, 'I am not trying to spook you, but seriously, there is a young man standing beside you.' She said she wasn't a psychic or a medium but sometimes she had clairvoyant feelings. 'I don't normally act on them, but this young man made me come over. I had no choice. He wants me to tell you that he is OK.'

I'm a natural sceptic but I think she was telling the truth. It didn't upset us; in fact, it made the island a better fit for us.

We spotted an apartment for sale and, on a whim, we put in an offer which was much lower than the asking price. The offer was accepted. The thing is we didn't have the money to buy it but we kept on postponing making the phone call to the agent cancelling our bid. We were keeping the dream alive, although we knew we couldn't go through with it. Couldn't afford to.

Days later, we were home again when two cheques land in the post, totalling £50,000. More than enough to put down a deposit.

It turns out that Stephen did join the pension scheme. This was it paying out because of his early death. We went ahead and bought the apartment and we still have it. There's a sign on the door, 'Stephen's Place'.

* *. *

Strange as it may seem, I also believe we have been in contact with Stephen, through a medium.

Martina knew about mediums; after her dad had died, she went to one. But I had zero faith in them, though that experience in the Majorcan bar had me thinking. Then a friend at work, Lee Buckingham, said, 'Why don't you speak to my brother?'

His brother, Ronnie Buckingham, is a medium. There was nothing to lose so an appointment was made.

Stephen was dead about five months when we first met Ronnie. A group of us went: me, Martina, Niall and Stephen's girlfriend, Claire. Ronnie held Martina's hand and then he went on to say: 'I have got a young chap here. Seventeen years old. He likes his name to be shortened in a way; it begins with the letter S. Steve.'

And then he looked at me and he said, 'The 4 February is very relevant to you and this boy.'

We were saying 'yes' to all of this, and then he said, 'He was killed in a car accident.'

I was never a sceptic again.

Over the following years Ronnie was in regular contact with us. I remember the time he phoned me at home just when I was having, what we'll call, a Stephen moment – sobbing, thinking about him while I was supposed to be painting the hall, stairs and landing.

The phone rang and it was Ronnie. He asked me why I was crying. He said Stephen had just told him to ring me and say, 'Look, I'm fine. There is not a problem.'

In all our time seeing him, he has never taken any money from us. I went to pay him the first day and he said, 'No. Because he's your child, I will not take any money. I charge people who just want a reading, but not people in your situation.'

Some time back, I had one last dream about Stephen. I know this might sound strange, but he was like a little mouse, with Stephen's head and face. I was holding him, cradling him, and he and I were talking but also crying. We were wading through a meandering stream which opened up to a wide estuary.

Suddenly, in an instant, he was gone from me. I was spinning around, desperate, then I saw him, skipping across the water and away. I have thought about that dream, and think it is about me finally letting go of Stephen, setting him free, and maybe, setting me free too.

* * *

There was one other death in my immediate family to cope with over this period. We learned in the spring of 2005 that my dear mother, Anna, was dying. I loved her to bits. She was an angel personified. She had fought and won a bout against cancer years before, but this time it was back and it held the winning hand.

I am the traditional Irish mother's son, the more so because I am of course the only boy. I could do no wrong. She had doted on me and had shown great love to Martina and the boys.

This was a difficult period and not helped because I was across the water in England. As her condition worsened, I found myself shuttling over to Dundalk every week. My work pattern of four days on, four days off helped. I'd head over at the end of the last run of shifts and stay there until the next was scheduled to begin.

She and Daddy had moved, for the duration, to my sister Eilish's home. No stairs to do battle with. It is a modern bungalow with great views of the shipping traffic in and out of Dundalk harbour and the Cooley Mountains beyond. Not a bad place to go for respite. We'd been told that there was no hope, but a decision was taken not to tell her of the doctor's prognosis because there was a little part of us that thought we could muster a miracle.

We'd go for drives or just sit together and talk. But towards the end Mammy was in pain, awful pain, and it seemed the morphine she was taking was having no effect.

The last day the whole family was there. I could sense from her breathing that she was struggling and I asked Daddy to light a candle. He lit it and held it in her hand. All us, Daddy and me and my sisters joined in prayer – 'Angel of God, my Guardian dear, to whom God's love commits me here, ever this day be at my side, to light and guard, to rule and guide. Amen.'

We wished that God would take her, to release her from her pain. We were telling her it was OK to go now. And she did go. She was at peace.

I didn't cry. I loved her so much but I didn't shed a tear. This still bothers me. I was just standing there, as if I was a neighbour helping the family, as if my mother meant nothing to me. Although deep down inside, it was killing me. I've thought about this and I think it's because compared to losing a child, losing a parent is a natural progression.

And I was, for want of a better term, played out after Stephen's death. I didn't have it in me emotionally the way I think I would have if things hadn't gone the way they did. Yes, I grieved, but I didn't cry. I just didn't have the capacity to release emotion. I think what had happened with Stephen had taken that from me.

Chapter 12
Family Tragedy, The Case Goes On

The family was reeling. It had been a tough couple of years. I was in a semi-permanent spin. Just when things got good or settled, they would go backwards. I was so lucky to have Martina at my side. Any other woman probably would have just said, 'Feck this – I am out of here', but she didn't. She stood by me all the way.

I looked at England differently after Stephen's death. I don't think I am alone in this, but when something as awful as a child's death happens you look for a reason, for some logic, for someone or something to blame. I was blaming God. I was blaming myself. I was blaming England. If we had stayed in Ireland, this wouldn't have happened.

England has been good to the family. Even though we landed here in the middle of the Troubles in the

1980s, only once have I ever felt an anti-Irish jibe. We were out one night with another Irish couple when we started getting some looks and then comments from a group of lads I thought looked like soldiers.

'We know where you are from. We know that border town.'

There was hostility in it, so I went up to the bar and ordered drinks as if we were intending to stay. I took them back to the table and we left quietly. That was the worst of it after more than twenty years here. But it wasn't home. Which is why we eventually took Stephen home. How we took him home is more convoluted.

* * *

Smyth's Norbertine Order attempted to deal with the aftermath of his crimes and their culpability in not stopping him, though I don't think this was ever decided in a civil court case because the cases were mostly negotiated. After selling the two farms in the 1990s, the Order settled seventeen cases. But there were more pending, including mine, though I also had a separate one running against the Church. The solicitors met and in 2005 they struck a one-off deal: each of the thirteen remaining claimants would receive

€68,000. The family of another victim who had died got €32,000.

To give credit to the Norbertine Order, there was an apology. And there was also an offer to meet me, in England or in Ireland. I didn't take the new Abbot, Fr Gerard Cusack, up on it, but the settlement came in useful.

The full details of the canonical inquiry I'd been involved in, back in 1975, hadn't yet been made public. Those details would have radically impacted on quite a few of the settlements, if they had been known, because some of these victims had been abused after 1975. There were survivors who made 'full and final settlements' which meant that all the new information in the world may be deemed irrelevant. You can't make a 'full and final settlement' twice, even if the new information seems to change everything.

My situation was slightly different because I was still suing the Church separately. That case had years to run.

* * *

Shortly afterwards, Martina and I were discussing ways of using the settlement money constructively. I didn't want to piss it up against the wall. And she turned to me and said – sort of in a statement – 'We are taking Stephen home.'

It made perfect sense, though it hadn't at the time Stephen died. We could bury him beside my mother in Dundalk, in a family plot. He could rest in peace with his own people. In Harlow he was on his own, in a place full of dead people, with no aunts or uncles or any relations there.

So we made enquiries. The exhumation was quite complicated and took three months to organise. Permission had to be sought to exhume, and then separate permission was needed to allow Stephen to be buried in Ireland. So the process began between funeral directors on both sides of the water. Everything had to be organised with military precision, with environmental health officials and the police involved.

The day came round, or rather the early morning because this was done at 4 a.m. Martina had flown across to Ireland the evening before. My brothers-in-law, Trevor and Jimmy, flew over from Ireland to be with me and Niall. Close friends were there also.

I remember how strange the whole process was. It was getting bright, but there was almost a dead silence, no bird song. Not a sound. And then suddenly there was lots of noise. The gravediggers were working behind a screen, so we couldn't see what was going on. But we could hear the original coffin being dragged up and pulled apart. Banging, cracking and smashing sounds. Stephen's coffin was placed into a special lead-lined casket, ready to transport to Ireland.

We met up again with the hearse when we all arrived at Heathrow for the flight home. As we were waiting to board the flight, through the window, I could see Stephen's casket on the apron being driven out and then pushed inside the hold of our plane. I blessed myself. I asked Niall, Trevor and Jimmy if they would mind if I sat on my own for the flight.

As the plane was taking off, I started talking to Stephen. I said, 'Say goodbye to England, Stephen. You will be home soon.' I chatted with him the whole way across, just as if he was sitting right next to me. And when we touched down in Dublin I said, 'Welcome to Ireland, son.'

I first thought something was wrong when I realised the undertaker wasn't there to meet us. Everything had been planned with that military precision. So where was he? I rang him and found out he hadn't even left Dundalk. He said Stephen wasn't due in for hours. I was giving out reams, telling him that Stephen was already here. Thirty minutes later, the undertaker arrived. That must have been the fastest hearse ever seen.

Off we go to the cargo area to collect Stephen and I spot the coffin, apparently heading off in the direction of County Carlow. I am about to go nuts until someone explains that Stephen is due in on the next flight. That was typical of Stephen, playing a wee joke on me, even at the very end.

We had another funeral mass, but this time we were more aware of what was going on around us, not like his first burial when we were stricken with grief. Later, Martina and I got to touch Stephen's coffin, and Niall got to carry his brother to his final resting place.

He is now buried next to my mammy in a double grave. The rules will allow us to go in with him when our time comes. In the meantime my sister Eilish keeps an eye on him. We call her his Irish mammy. She tends the grave and makes sure there are fresh flowers.

* * *

We worried about Niall afterwards. He quit football when Stephen died. He wouldn't play; he stopped everything. It was a month or so before I noticed, and then realised that he just didn't have the head to do it. Whatever was going on inside him, he just couldn't do it.

Football was both their lives. But there was no way I was going to push him back into it. It was something I thought about really deep and hard. So we waited until he actually got back into it himself two or three years later. He plays for two teams now, one on a Saturday and one on a Sunday.

Martina had him as if he was in a glass box. He couldn't go to the toilet on his own; she was watching every move he made. Eventually that eased. It had to. On both our parts. But you can imagine how terrified we were when he started taking driving lessons.

Since then he has done well. After school, he went straight into a job at a heating and gas suppliers shop, where he is yet. Level-headed. And he got himself a lovely girl too, Sara. They were old school friends when they got together as a couple. Not long after they became an official item, Niall came home and told Martina that they were expecting.

Martina had known Sara for years and loved her and was totally chuffed, but Niall was unsure how I would take it. He was so anxious that he got Martina to phone me and tell me.

He needn't have worried. I was delighted. I was going to be a grandparent – magic!

Did I think of old Ireland? Yes. And I realised how things had changed for the better. The hypocrisy was gone. Back in the day, not that long ago, our grandchild might have been given up for adoption. Baby Frankie was born in December 2010. A great wee man.

* * *

By then, there had been very significant developments in my case against the Church. Fr John B. Brady's career path had taken him a long way since 1975. First to Rome and the Irish College, then to the Archbishop's palace in Armagh when he became the Primate of All Ireland in 1996 and finally, in 2007, to the post of Cardinal. As the head of the Armagh Archdiocese, in which I had lived, he was named in my law suit. Others too had named him in their papers.

I was told not to be too optimistic about the outcome. So much time had passed, it might be time-barred and proving that the Irish Church, as opposed to the Norbertines, had charge over Smyth would be difficult, if not impossible. I thought the strongest element of the case was the evidence that the Church had failed to act properly after the canonical inquiry in 1975 to ensure that Smyth never harmed anyone again.

It was just before March 2010 that the break-through came. There'd been developments in the case of another victim of Smyth. She had been abused before and, crucially, after the canonical inquiry in 1975. Her name was Marie McCormack.

I had met her at the sentencing of Smyth in Dublin, in 1997, and had stayed in touch, though she lived in Canada. I knew she was suing the Norber-tine Order, the Diocese of Kilmore and Cardinal Seán Brady as head of the Catholic Church and in his personal capacity.

What I didn't know was that in 2007 her legal team, headed by solicitor Brian Coady, had got possession of the records of the canonical inquiry of 1975. They used them to file their case in the Irish High Court. In March, the *Sunday Independent* got sight of them from the court records and a huge story broke.

The gist of the story was the same as was published in the *Sunday Mirror* thirteen years earlier, but there was much more detail. Included in the new informa-tion was the fact that two children had been questioned and that they had each been sworn not to speak about the process. Although the High Court never formally ruled on the matter, the astonishing element was the specific allegations against Cardinal Brady.

This is what Cardinal Brady (the second named defendant) was accused of:

1. Failing to report to An Garda Síochána the fact of formal signed complaints against Father Brendan Smyth of sexual assault and paedophilia on other children, made to the Church authorities and investigated by them at interviews, at which the Second Named Defendant was present and participated, held in Dundalk and Ballyjamesduff on the 29th March 1975 and the 4th April 1975 respectively.

2. Failing, following such interviews, to take any or any adequate steps to ensure that Father Brendan Smyth did not continue to perpetrate sexual assaults on children including the Plaintiff.

3. Requiring and causing the two children the subject matter of the inquiries held on the 29th March 1975 and the 4th April 1975 to sign, under oath, undertakings that they would not discuss their interview with anyone except priests who had permission to discuss it.

4. By failing in his duty to report the complaints against Father Brendan Smyth, negligently deprived the Plaintiff and others of appropriate medical treatment.

I'm no legal expert, but it was clear to me that this was an important development.

The Church spokesman put out a statement in response saying that Cardinal Brady had acted at the direction of his Bishop, Francis McKiernan, as the 'recording secretary for the process involved'. At the second 'meeting' the Church said Cardinal Brady had 'asked the questions and recorded the answers given'.

The statement continued: 'At those meetings the complainants signed undertakings, on oath, to respect the confidentiality of the information gathering process. As instructed, and as a matter of urgency, Fr Brady passed both reports to Bishop McKiernan for his immediate action.'

Well, you can imagine the response to all of this. Cardinal Brady was put under all sorts of pressure. He himself spoke to the media, in Armagh, that same Sunday. He was clear that he didn't think this was a resigning matter and said:

'I insist again I did act and acted effectively in

that inquiry to produce the grounds for removing Fr Smyth from ministry and specifically, it was under-lined, that he was not to hear confessions and that was very important.'

He also said he was not the designated authority to report to the Garda and that Smyth's Norbertine Order was responsible for the priest.

There were calls for the Cardinal to resign or to consider his position. This wouldn't be the last time such calls would be made.

A couple of days later, on St Patrick's Day, he made a considered statement: 'This week a painful episode from my own past has come before me. I have listened to reaction from people to my role in events thirty-five years ago. I want to say to anyone who has been hurt by any failure on my part that I apologise to you with all my heart. I also apologise to all those who feel I have let them down. Looking back, I am ashamed that I have not always upheld the values that I profess and believe in.'

He also said that he intended to do much reflec-tion. Fair enough. But whatever reflection he made, it didn't lead him to believe his position as head of the Irish Catholic Church was untenable. He stayed in his post.

Later that year, in June, Marie McCormack agreed a settlement shortly before her case was supposed to go to trial. No figures were ever made public, but a sum of approximately €300,000 was reported.

She got three apologies: from the Cardinal, the Bishop of Kilmore and the Norbertine Order. Neither the diocese nor Cardinal Brady accepted liability, but the Norbertines put their hands up. They admitted that after Smyth's ordination in 1951 'on many occasions during the following 40 years he was subject to complaints and suspicions with regard to the sexual abuse of children'. And they also conceded that the measures taken to prevent him harming children were 'seriously inadequate'. Finally, they accepted that they'd 'failed to implement the disciplinary steps which his conduct demanded'.

Marie never said a word about it – I think she was subject to a confidentiality clause.

* * *

My own case carried on slowly. You'd imagine that the McCormack case and mine were tied together but they weren't. Smyth had continued to abuse her after the canonical inquiry, whereas my sexual abuse stopped then. In fact, my solicitor only received the records of the canonical inquiry that autumn, thirteen years after we had asked for them.

I glanced at them. It was almost too much for me to read. So much of that evening came flooding back. Me, alone. And my father outside the door. And the fear and terror as I was being quizzed. It was the invasive nature of the questions that hit me, that and the oath. My childish signature. How on earth was that appropriate? Any of it?

What I didn't do, and, to my knowledge, no one else did, was actually investigate what Cardinal Brady did with the information I had given them. This was the first time since the inquiry that I was aware of the detail I had furnished the Church. All those names and addresses that I had given. And all the information that the other boy, who I have called Cavan Boy, gave.

But the real significance of this didn't sink in. Even though I knew from the 1997 trial that Belfast Boy's family were unaware that I had taken part in the canonical inquiry, I didn't make the logical conclusion – that those children that I had named hadn't been warned. Not then.

Meanwhile, I had finished the last of a series of psychiatric evaluations. One report concluded I was suffering from post-traumatic stress disorder (PTSD).

This was tied to revelations that Smyth had continued to abuse after 1975 and my guilt in not bringing it to an effective end. Another psychiatrist said that wasn't the case but that I was suffering from 'chronic adjustment order with anxiety'. He explained this related to the abuse generally, the re-exposure to the abuse in the 1990s and my reaction to the continuing legal case. A swift end to proceedings would help me, he said.

I was grateful for the reports, even if they differed, because they proved something was going on in my head apart from my imagination.

Legal correspondence was coming through the letterbox much more often, a sure sign, I was told, that things were coming to a head. Into 2011 and I was confident that things would end sooner rather than later – later, as it turned out. There were several court dates mentioned before one was finally fixed for the end of November.

Once you get a court date, negotiations start, or so it seems in cases like these which are hardly ever fought out in the court room. The two legal teams began talking about a week or so before the date. My solicitor rang with their first offer, which he said was ridiculous, €10,000 with me paying my legal fees too, which would have left me in a very deep black hole.

Then it stepped up to €50,000, but now I was getting the hang of this horse trading and I said, 'Don't ring me back, because I will not take anything less than €100,000 with the legal fees on top.'

I was happy to go to court and fight it out. I knew what side justice was on, though equally my legal team had always made clear it could go any way at all in court. There were no guarantees.

It took two days, but eventually I got the call. I had held out and got what I wanted.

Around about this time, my solicitor got a call from a BBC journalist who was trying to contact me about the case, something about taking part in a documentary. He'd spotted my case on the High Court diary and didn't know it had been settled. I wasn't interested.

30 November came around and, instead of a high court battle, my solicitor went to Dublin's Four Courts, confirming that a settlement had been reached with the Church, in fact officially with the Armagh Archdiocese, and then released a statement on my behalf. I had written it and then asked him to read it over, to make sure it was legally watertight, and amend accordingly.

I made the point that, despite assurances that me and my family had been given, Smyth had been able to abuse other children after the canonical inquiry. I reminded anyone who wanted to know that at Smyth's trial I had met other victims ten to fifteen years younger than me who would not have been abused if the assurances given had been honoured. I felt responsible for their misery. My guilt plagued me.

There was no admission of liability nor an apology on the terms I wanted. I had asked for Cardinal Brady to publicly acknowledge and accept the failings of the Church in its handling of the circumstances which gave rise to the case and to apologise for them. That didn't happen.

Cardinal Brady was happy to meet in private and apologise; that was the method he considered appropriate. Me, I considered any private meeting to be inappropriate. There was far too much water under this particular bridge for a chat over a cup of tea and biscuits to be sufficient.

The settlement made the news as you'd expect. My statement got a fair run-out and I was satisfied with that. I was asked to do a TV interview but I wasn't ready for that. I did agree, though, to do one radio interview. I did it in a studio in London with an RTÉ reporter, Colm Ó Mongáin, in Dublin chatting to me down the line. That went very well.

It was pre-recorded, which suited me perfectly. The reporter edited it and played it back to me, so I knew what was going to be broadcast.

Afterwards, I got a lot of good feedback from family and friends in Ireland. I am not a wildly confident person. Shy, at least at first, might be a good description. So the positive reaction was great. The phone was hopping with texts. And all were agreed it had been worth doing, but I had no intention of saying anything else.

* * *

Then, a day or so later, I got a call from my sister Eilish. The *Irish Independent* had published an apology about their coverage of the story.

This is what the paper wrote:

'In reference to a story in yesterday's *Irish Independent*, we have been asked to clarify that Cardinal Seán Brady, then Fr Seán Brady, did not make Brendan Boland take an oath in 1975. Whilst he witnessed the statement of Brendan Boland, Fr Brady's role was as note-taker in this Church inquiry team charged with bringing a case against Fr Brendan Smyth.'

Well, that took the biscuit! This was wordplay gone mad. I knew that Cardinal Brady had sworn me to secrecy because his name was down in black and white beside my own. He had administered it, just as he had done with Cavan Boy. Did he make me do it in the sense that he tied me up, and forced a pen into my hand? No. But he definitely oversaw it, and countersigned it.

The Church was flexing its muscles again. You know people say it has lost lots of its power, but I'm not so sure. My truth was being undermined. It was making me out to be a liar because, in my own statement, I had specifically pointed out Cardinal Brady's role in the oath.

As angry as I was, I didn't know how to put this right. Would the newspaper issue a counter-apology? I didn't think so. So I rang my solicitor:

'About the correction in the paper, do you still have a number for that bloke you said was doing a programme on the BBC?'

Of course he had it. So I phoned and got through to BBC journalist Darragh MacIntyre. Before we got further than introductions, he asked me to hold on a second while he parked up. He'd been driving over a mountain in Donegal. Two or three minutes later, I'd agreed to meet him, over here, in England, but I made it clear this could only be a chat, no promises and no interview.

That was the start of getting the full story out, without corrections or clarifications.

Chapter 13
The BBC Investigate

I arranged to meet the BBC team a few days later, close to my home not far from Stansted Airport. I had no intention of making a TV programme. I just wanted to get a sense of what these people were doing and to see if maybe I could contribute, to see if my story had any relevance to them, and if they had any relevance to me.

Martina was supportive. She knew how annoyed I was at the retractions in the newspaper and, though she has never said this, was probably worried that I might slip back into my fog of guilt. I was starting to become much more resilient in the months leading up to the settlement and I'd been on a high in the days around it. I suppose she thought things might go backwards.

That wasn't going to happen. I had resolved to take charge of my new life and instead of things being done to me, instead of me being the victim, I was going to try to keep control of the situation. Easier said than done, of course.

Naturally, knowing my track record, I managed a minor mishap. I'd scheduled to meet the BBC at a pub restaurant for lunch. However it wasn't open when we arrived just before noon. It was a freezing cold day. Snow in the air. Not the sort of day to hang about outside. So then it was a case of keeping eyes trained around the car park to catch the BBC team and explain. Sure enough, one lost-looking pair landed and we met, spending the next fifteen minutes in our car, chatting.

Fifteen minutes later, when the place eventually opened, we all sat down for a bite to eat. Time to suss them out. The two of them, director Alison Millar and reporter Darragh MacIntyre, took time to explain what they were doing, a current affairs TV documentary for the BBC2's *This World* series. They were making a programme about Ireland's clerical abuse controversy. Already they had spent time in Donegal, examining the aftermath and consequences of an infamous clerical paedophile case but were planning a wider film, which would look at how the Church was coping and how the people of a once very Catholic Ireland had been affected.

I had heard of Darragh before because of his work with the BBC *Panorama* programme, which I watched regularly. He was an experienced investigative reporter. Alison, I found out, had a very strong record as a documentary maker, including a film about Fr Michael Cleary, the singing priest, who had two children with his housekeeper. They were serious film makers. They reminded me how the Irish Taoiseach Enda Kenny had lambasted the Catholic Church in the Dáil because of its problems and failings dealing with abuse. He had been speaking as yet another inquiry into clerical abuse published its report – this time it concerned the Cloyne diocese in Cork. Its conclusions were, as ever, damning.

The Taoiseach had read into the record:

The revelations of the Cloyne Report have brought the Government, Irish Catholics and the Vatican to an unprecedented juncture.

It's fair to say that after the Ryan and Murphy Reports Ireland is, perhaps, unshockable when it comes to the abuse of children. But Cloyne has proved to be of a different order.

Because, for the first time in this country, a report into child sexual-abuse exposes an attempt by the Holy See to frustrate an Inquiry in a sovereign, democratic republic as little as three years ago, not three decades ago (this was a reference to the Vatican's lack of cooperation with the investigators. One of the issues that they wanted to clarify was Vatican edicts to an Irish bishop which could be interpreted as an invitation to cover up abuse).

And in doing so, the Cloyne Report excavates the dysfunction, the disconnection, the elitism that dominate the culture of the Vatican to this day.

The rape and torture of children were downplayed or 'managed', to uphold instead the primacy of the institution, its power, its standing and its 'reputation'.

This is the Republic of Ireland 2011, a republic of laws, of rights and responsibilities, of proper civic order, where the delinquency and the arrogance of a particular version of a particular kind of 'morality' will no longer be tolerated or ignored.

As a practising Catholic, I don't say any of this easily. Growing up, many of us in here learned that we were part of a pilgrim Church. Today, that Church needs to be a penitent Church, a Church truly and deeply penitent for the horrors it perpetrated, that it hid and that it denied.

Months later, the Irish government closed down its dedicated embassy to the Vatican. These were still major talking points at home, but living in England they had fallen right off my radar.

Martina and I listened. This was all about seeing if we could trust these people and also to see if this was to be a serious film and not some sensational piece of journalism. We knew that, if we didn't like what we were hearing, we could just make our excuses and leave. This meeting had been organised with no conditions, except one: everything was off record until such time as we agreed it wasn't. And there were no cameras.

As it happened we got along fine. The four of us were all of-an-age and could make small talk about football or music when the story of my personal experience of abuse was getting uncomfortable. We were about two hours in to the meeting, the meal eaten and the dishes cleared, when I made a decision. I'd show them the documents, all of the records from the canonical inquiry. I had brought them with me but I had left them in the car in case the meeting went badly.

I went and got them, handed them to Darragh, and headed outside for a cigarette with Martina and Alison. He buried himself in the documents and we kept clear for the next ten minutes.

When we came back in, he said to me, 'Do you realise what you have here?'

And I didn't. Not a clue. Because even though I had had them for a while, since the previous September, I had not examined them in detail. I didn't even like looking at them, and when I did, it only reminded me of how pitiful and useless I felt I had been.

Darragh had gone straight to the transcriptions of my questioning at the canonical inquiry, but instead of focusing on the material which directly related to me, he had spotted what I had forgotten about for so long – those names which I had given to the inquiry of children that had been abused by Smyth or who had been along on trips with Smyth and might have been abused.

I allowed him to take some of the papers away to copy. There was still no agreement about what I might do with them in the programme. I was prepared to help but was very nervous about taking it much further than the paperwork. Forty-eight hours later, the original documents were returned to me intact. Another meeting was organised.

By now Darragh had gone through the documents line by line, paying particular attention to the material in the handwriting of Cardinal Brady, where Brady outlined how he got involved in the canonical inquiry.

He pointed to the phrase, 'I was despatched to investigate the complaint'. Cardinal Brady was not simply the 'note-taker', he was an investigator.

I began to give serious consideration to taking part in the film. At first, I thought of just doing a voice-only interview. I was afraid of people in England, my workmates and my neighbours, learning about the abuse. That might seem odd, given I had already been interviewed on radio in Ireland and my name was out there, but I didn't want the story following me around in England. If the film was to be shown only in Ireland, on BBC Northern Ireland, I thought I could live with that, but the problem was this was going to be shown across the UK on BBC2. For certain, some of my workmates would see it and I didn't know how they would react.

Many people who have survived sexual abuse will say the same thing. Suffering from sexual abuse can leave you with an injury much more grievous than, say, a broken leg, but who wants to talk about it, or look for sympathy? At best, it's an embarrassing wound, and at its worst, well, it kick-starts feelings of guilt or even complicity. Put simply, you have to really think it's worth it before you put your head above the parapet.

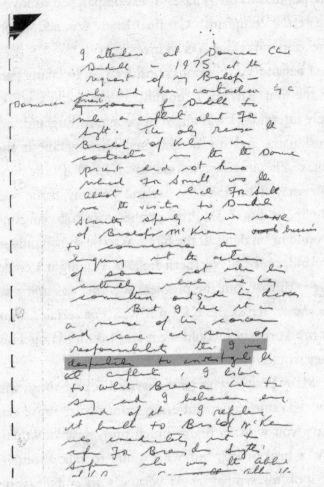

This document in Cardinal Seán Brady's handwriting is not dated. It was held in Catholic Church files and released (along with all the Church's notes and transcriptions of both 1975 interviews) to Brendan Boland's legal team in 2010. The key phrase: 'I was despatched to investigate' has been highlighted.

Transcription

I attended at Dominican Church Dundalk in 1975 at the request of my Bishop – who had been contacted by a Dominican priest from Dundalk to make a complaint about Fr [Brendan] Smyth. The only reason the Bishop of Kilmore was contacted was that the Dominican priest did not know which Fr Smith was the Abbot and which Fr Smith was the visitor to Dundalk. Strictly speaking it was none of Bishop McKiernan's business to commission an inquiry about the activities of someone not under his authority which were being committed outside his diocese.

But I believe it is a measure of his concern and care and sense of responsibility that I was despatched to investigate the complaint. I listened to what Brendan had to say and I believed every word of it. I referred it back to Bishop McKiernan who immediately sent the information [to] Fr Brendan Smyth's superior who was the Abbot [of Kilnacrott, Abbot Kevin Smith]

A third meeting, this time at Stansted Airport, just before Christmas, decided me about the interview. There were choices offered. My face could be blacked out in some way. I think one idea was to interview me behind a window with water running down it and to camouflage my voice too. But it was also explained to me that speaking directly to the camera is the best way to present your case. This I understood. There are times when I have seen people interviewed in silhouette and I am not sure if they are the good guy or the bad guy. That thought made up my mind: I was ready for the stage.

Already I had been persuaded that this programme would do more than scratch the surface. I wanted to state my case and to explain exactly how I was treated. Also, I wanted to help other victims of sexual abuse, not just clerical abuse, because, as is now clear, much sexual abuse occurs in family circles or is perpetrated by 'trusted' friends.

It was at this meeting that Martina made one decisive contribution. She wondered aloud if the parents of Cavan Boy, the other Smyth child victim interviewed in the process in 1975, had been told what happened to him.

I remember the BBC team thinking this was worth following up. They had already asked if I was happy for them to use the names and addresses that I had given the Church all those years ago, to see if they could find out what had happened to them. I think they were hoping to confirm, one way or the other, if these children had also been abused. I don't think they really imagined that their families hadn't been warned and the children not protected. The biggest shock they got was in the case of Cavan Boy.

He was fifteen when he was questioned by Fr Brady. He told them that his parents were told nothing about his involvement in this secret Church investigation. More than that, he said his parents were not told that he was being abused by Fr Brendan Smyth. The Church of course said nothing and he said nothing to anyone, not to a soul, because he was sworn to secrecy about the process, just like me.

Over the next month or so, the documentary team tracked down all those I had named. In the case of Belfast Boy, who like me and Cavan Boy had been abused while on trips with Smyth, they were able to find his family at the same address I had given for him in 1975. The children, now adults, had one thing in common: their families had been told absolutely nothing about Smyth. None of them. The Church had their names and their addresses but chose not to alert the parents about Smyth and the obvious danger he posed.

In fact, four of the five children that I had told the inquiry about, and who were named in the transcript, had been abused by Smyth. One of them, a girl from Cavan, was abused after 1975. Belfast Boy was abused for another year. His sister, who I recall telling the inquiry about, was abused for another seven years. Their four first cousins were abused, in turn, right up until 1988. All it would have taken to spare these children abuse was to warn the parents. A phone call. A house visit.

One child, who I have called Belfast Girl, had been spared. Smyth had never made a move on her. I remembered her as very pretty and outgoing. Psychologists might be able to figure that out. Perhaps she was stronger in some way than us others, maybe not so deferential. Certainly she was the most confident of us all.

* * *

When the time came to do my interview, I was nervous. I was involved in an almost physical struggle to overpower my natural shyness. But I was also committed to what I saw as truth telling and I knew I had to get my story out there, clearly and succinctly. We sat down, Darragh and I, in the living room of the lovely home of my sister Eilish and brother-in-law Trevor, in Dundalk. We got underway. I hardly noticed the cameraman, Séamus McCracken, even though he had turned the room into a TV studio for the afternoon.

And so it went. I calmed down and spoke for the best part of a couple of hours. I can't say it was all easy chit-chat, but it wasn't as difficult as I had imagined. I discovered a fluency that I don't always have in public, the sort of fluency my Stephen had. He seemed present with me that day. I had taken time to visit with him at the cemetery on the old Newry Road and was glad I did.

I was told it had gone well. But what did that mean? I had nothing to compare it with. The radio interview had been over so quickly; this was an entirely different experience. Draining. A head melter. But it was also very satisfying. I knew I had made the points I wanted to make. There were questions that I wanted answered now. What was going to happen next? Was Cardinal Brady going to do an interview? How would the film eventually turn out? These questions couldn't be answered then, and I had one more part to play.

Belfast Boy had decided to do an interview for the programme, but this was problematic. He was happy to be interviewed normally but was anxious that he didn't compromise the privacy of his sister and his extended family, who had been abused too. All this I learned later, after I had an extraordinary meeting with him myself.

I was asked would I like to meet him? It was explained that ideally the meeting would be filmed. Was I happy with that? No problem. This was someone who I had shared a life-defining experience with years ago. We had had no contact since we were dropped off by Smyth, after our overnight visit to Dublin and The Wombles' concert in 1975. I'd been told that life hadn't run very smoothly for him since. He'd been married and divorced; used to drink too much. But things were going OK for him now. Arrangements were made to meet in the seaside town of Holywood in County Down. It might have been simpler to meet in a café and then do an interview about it later but the plan was to film us meeting as it actually happened. No interviews. Just to let the two of us meet up and see where our chat went.

I remember the biting wind as I waited on a coastal path for Belfast Boy to arrive. I was standing looking out to sea. It was freezing and the wind was howling, and then I could hear the cameraman saying, 'He is coming now. He is coming now.'

The next thing, I see a shadow coming towards me and I turn round and it's Belfast Boy, and he has his hood up. I just looked at him and went, 'Hello, buddy', and threw my arms around him. Everything happened then in a really natural way. We hugged and talked like lifelong friends.

For me, it was the completion of a circle. Both of us had been through a fair amount of shite but we'd survived and hopefully were stronger for it. We discovered that, apart from the experience of being abused, we also had at least one other thing in common – we both loved music. Belfast Boy had been playing in bands for years and did gigs up and down the island, including in my hometown of Dundalk: Folk Rock. He told me about his tin whistle and fiddle. I told him about my guitars. A truly special day.

* * *

Some weeks later, we got together again to watch the film before it was broadcast. It was called *The Shame of the Catholic Church*. I tried to detach myself from it, as if it wasn't me that was in it, but it was very difficult because I knew the story inside out. My interview had been cut back from two hours to a few minutes, but I think these excerpts get my point across. I explained how I told the canonical inquiry the details of the abuse that I knew about:

I'd given them the names of the other children that were with me on the trips … There was a boy from Belfast, I gave them his name and address; there was a girl from Belfast, I gave them her name and address; there was a girl from Cavan, I gave them her name and address. And there was another boy from Cavan, I gave them his name and address. And there was another boy that was his friend.

I told them that I witnessed one boy being abused … That was the boy from Belfast. I knew for a fact he was abused and the other boy from Cavan, he told me he was abused 'cos he didn't like going on the trips either.

Belfast Boy's interview in the film was heart-stopping. He was filmed off camera but in his own voice. He said:

I remember going up to Dublin with Brendan. I think there were about five or six of us on that trip.

Brendan was a nice fellow – he was probably as petrified as I was at the time.

In many ways I felt very guilty too – you know – sharing a room with this other boy, Smyth and his behaviour and what he wanted us to do, and the way he wanted us to behave. It's unbearable to think about it sometimes, you know.

And then as it transpired that Brendan had mentioned me, and that my name and address was actually on these documents as well.

It's like a knife into your chest … just like a sudden sharp pain.

Nobody came to our house – they should have come to our house and warned our family, or my parents and said look, this is what's happening. This man is involved in this. We would strictly advise you to keep him away from the house.

Okay, maybe I only had another year's abuse to go, but my sister, for years after that she was abused and then, lo and behold, cousins after that.

Belfast Boy's interview was devastating and it went right to the heart of the matter. You see this wasn't about going to the gardaí or the police, not even about going to the social services. This was about a simple warning: 'Your man isn't safe with children. Keep yours well away from him.'

That never happened. And so the abuse continued against Belfast Boy, and then his younger sister for another seven years and his four first cousins in turn.

* * *

The film analysed the role of Cardinal Brady and asked why he and the Catholic Church seemed to minimise his role, calling him a note-taker and a notary without powers who did his duty, when it was plain that he had been tasked with the investigation into Smyth. The film revealed that key line from Cardinal Brady, the one Darragh had mined from the documentation: 'I was despatched to investigate the complaint.'

There was also an excerpt from an interview that Cardinal Brady had given RTÉ, in 2009, about what he would do if he found that a child had been abused as a result of any managerial failure on his part. He said: 'If I found myself in the situation where I was aware that my failure to act had allowed or meant that other children were abused, well, then I think I would resign.'

Cardinal Brady declined the opportunity of a proper sit-down interview with the BBC, which led to an exchange between him and Darragh in Limerick, in a so-called door-step interview. This is most of it as broadcast:

'Hello, Darragh MacIntyre, BBC. Cardinal Brady, I'd like to ask you a couple of questions, if you don't mind?'

'No, no. I am … thanks very much … but … I am not ready.'

'Cardinal Brady, you said that you would resign if you thought any actions of yours had led to a child being abused. You know that children were abused, because you failed, in part, because you failed to protect them.'

'I did what I was there to do. I gathered the evidence.'

'You had the names of and addresses, Cardinal, of children who were abused or who were at risk of being abused and you did not protect them.'

Cardinal Brady ignored that question and two other questions on the same theme. As far as I was concerned, all the questions were on the mark. For goodness sake, he had gone and got the information; he had done the hard work. All he had to do was make sure his boss, the Bishop of Kilmore, acted properly with it.

Certainly, the Bishop of Kilmore should have ensured that the families were warned, but it's not as if Cardinal Brady was unaware of what had been done. He was the Bishop's secretary at the time. He also knew exactly what *wasn't done*. He was a school teacher too, remember? What was he thinking?

There is no doubt that Cardinal Brady took great comfort from the fact that Smyth's right to hear Confession had been suspended. There were other restrictions on Smyth's public priestly duties, but I can't see that any of them really impacted on his career as an abuser or as a priest.

The BBC found pictures of Smyth helping at a special mass for the sick at Knock in 1979, four years after he was punished. That mass was headed by then Bishop Cahal Daly, who twelve years later would become Cardinal Daly.

Chapter 14
No More Secrets

After seeing the film this first time, before it was broadcast, I decided it was time to start telling people about my secret. The story was going to be on national television and whatever impact it made there was a chance my mates, Martina's mates and our neighbours would see it.

I had a very simple way of doing this at work. I'd go up to so and so, and say, 'By the way, do me a favour, type in Brendan Boland and Seán Brady in Google and see what comes up.' Then I'd head out for a cigarette. That was my way of telling people.

There was nothing but support. One bloke was upset when I came back in. When he realised what had happened and who I was battling against, what position he had in the Church, he just couldn't believe it. As far as he was concerned, it would be like taking on Queen Elizabeth II as the Head of the Church.

He gave off to me for not telling people sooner and told me that everyone would only have been interested in offering support. There would have been no name-calling or whispered nonsense about me. He was right: all I got at work and at home was kindness and understanding.

* * *

The programme was broadcast on 1 May 2012. I watched it at home with Martina by my side. There was excitement and fear when we sat down. I'd seen the film, but there had been a few changes since the viewing in Belfast and, of course, no matter what I thought, there was the reaction from everyone else to worry about.

In the middle of that muddle of emotions, of fear and excitement, there was sadness; sadness at the loss of my innocence, sadness at the price that Martina and the children had paid for all that had happened, sadness thinking how things might have been better.

So as the programme was playing live on the TV in my living room, I cried. So did Martina.

The film began with the story of Fr Eugene Greene, a priest who had terrorised children for decades in Donegal in the north-west of the island. The abuse had been covered up. Instead of stopping him, he'd been moved from parish to parish. Belatedly, the Church admitted that 'significant errors of judgement had been made by successive bishops'.

Halfway through, the film switched focus onto me, Smyth and the role of Cardinal Brady. It ended with a moment from the meeting I had with Belfast Boy by the sea. We were walking side by side, when I said to him, 'I thought I'd saved you.'

I said much more than that of course but that was the line that was used in the film. I didn't intend it to have significance when I said it, but it was the truth: I had tried to save them all.

But I wasn't allowed to be maudlin for too long. The instant the programme ended, the phones went mad. Texts, calls, e-mails, Facebook ... The support was unbelievable, incredible. And proof that it had been worthwhile, me taking part in the programme. Some wanted just to say, well done, others wanted to apologise as Catholics for what had happened to me, and still others wanted to congratulate me, telling me I was very brave.

But I don't think I was brave. I have always said that I just told the truth. There is nothing difficult about it, nothing brave about it: I just told the truth. Others should have told the truth years earlier and none of this would have happened.

* * *

There was a concern that the programme might be discounted as just another film on the Irish clerical sex-abuse scandal. There'd been dozens since Chris Moore's exposé on Smyth in 1994. Maybe the audience was tired of the subject; after all, it was no secret that the Church had covered up for abusers in its ranks.

Technically, the film wasn't shown in the Irish Republic, but, nevertheless, it was watched by many thousands because the vast majority of homes there can view the BBC. And the BBC showed it on consecutive nights, first on BBC Northern Ireland, then on BBC2 across the UK. Both broadcasts were picked up south of the border.

Television is a powerful thing. My story was beamed into the homes of the nation and, even if you were minded to try and ignore it, you couldn't ignore the headlines which followed. I set off news stories and commentaries which ran for the best part of two weeks across Ireland. I hadn't guessed at this at all.

Cardinal Brady was under pressure to resign again. Politicians on both sides of the border spoke up about it.

On 4 May 2012, Harry McGee reported in *The Irish Times*:

Political leaders from across the party spectrum have called on Dr Seán Brady to consider his position following allegations that he failed to pass on information about the activities of notorious paedophile priest Brendan Smyth.

Senior figures, including Taoiseach Enda Kenny, Tánaiste Eamon Gilmore and the leaders of all the major parties, have responded to the disclosures in a BBC documentary by indicating it raises questions as to the cardinal's tenability as Primate of All-Ireland.

The BBC *This World* documentary, *The Shame of the Catholic Church*, disclosed how a Church inquiry in 1975 involving Dr Brady, then a priest, was given the names and addresses of children who Smyth abused. This information was never given to the children's parents or gardaí.

Mr Gilmore said it was the State's job to enact laws and to ensure those laws applied to everybody, whether they belonged to a church or not. 'It is my own personal view that anybody who did not deal with the scale of the abuse we have seen in this case should not hold a position of authority,' he told the Dáil.

The Taoiseach stopped short of calling for Dr Brady to consider his position. He said, however, that the cardinal should 'reflect' on the outcome of the programme.

Asked if he believed the cardinal should resign, Mr Kenny said he was in a 'different position' than others, as he was head of Government, but said his views were well known.

Minister for Education Ruairi Quinn said the Catholic Church, as patron of 92 per cent of Irish primary schools, needed to ask itself was Dr Brady a suitable person to be its head in Ireland.

'I think anybody who is aware that a crime had been committed against young men, a crime of rape, and who, at the time, no matter what else was going on, did not report that to the gardaí, in the light of what has since happened, I think really should consider their position,' said Mr Quinn.

Fianna Fáil leader Micheál Martin echoed the sentiment, saying the enormity and scale of

Smyth's abuse of young children in very vulnerable circumstances meant Dr Brady should consider his position. 'His authority has been very seriously undermined by what has happened.'

The North's Deputy First Minister Martin McGuinness said when the issue first emerged two years ago, he had said Dr Brady should consider his position. He said many Catholics would be 'dismayed' at the new allegations and Dr Brady should reflect on his stated position that he will stay on as leader of his Church in Ireland.

SDLP leader Alasdair McDonnell said Dr Brady had in 2010 set out criteria for judging when he should resign over failure to act. 'In the minds of many Catholics, those criteria have been met,' he said.

Cardinal Brady has criticised elements of the documentary and complained it 'deliberately exaggerated' his role as a member of a 1975 Church inquiry team. He has claimed his role was confined to that of notary or note taker. He also said the programme makers had not carried the verdict of a senior Vatican investigation exonerating his role.

He said he would not be standing down over the issue but acknowledged: 'I was part of an unhelpful culture of deference and silence in society, and the Church, which thankfully is now a thing of the past.'

Last night, professor emeritus of moral theology at St Patrick's College Maynooth Fr Vincent Twomey said Cardinal Brady should resign. Speaking on RTÉ's *Prime Time* programme, he said he 'had unfortunately lost his moral credibility'.

Fr Twomey queried: 'Where is the humanity, the imagination that can't realise that these children have suffered so much? For the good of the Church, I'm afraid I am of the opinion that I think he should resign.'

I was asked my opinion and I gave it.

How could Cardinal Brady have any moral authority as the leader of Irish Catholics when he had clearly let down us children all those years ago? All the excuses in the world couldn't excuse why he and the Church didn't just go and tell those families what Smyth was doing to their children. And I asked again, as I had when my case was settled six months earlier, for a public apology. None came.

Cardinal Brady's spokesmen repeated what they had said two years earlier: that Cardinal Brady had done his job in 1975. He had passed the information he had got up to his superiors. In a statement put out in the immediate aftermath of the programme Cardinal Brady said:

> To suggest, as the programme does, that I led the investigation of the 1975 Church Inquiry into allegations against Brendan Smyth is seriously misleading and untrue. I was asked by my then Bishop (Bishop Francis McKiernan of the Diocese of Kilmore) to assist others who were more senior to me in this Inquiry process on a one-off basis only.
>
> The documentation of the interview with Brendan Boland, signed in his presence, clearly identifies me as the 'notary' or 'note-taker'. Any suggestion that I was other than a 'notary' in the process of recording evidence from Mr Boland is false and misleading.
>
> I did not formulate the questions asked in the Inquiry process. I did not put these questions to Mr Boland. I simply recorded the answers that he gave.
>
> Acting promptly and with the specific purpose of corroborating the evidence provided by Mr Boland, thereby strengthening the case against

Brendan Smyth, I subsequently interviewed one of the children identified by Mr Boland who lived in my home diocese of Kilmore. That I conducted this interview on my own is already on the public record. This provided prompt corroboration of the evidence given by Mr Boland.

In 1975 no State or Church guidelines existed in the Republic of Ireland to assist those responding to an allegation of abuse against a minor. No training was given to priests, teachers, police officers or others.

In fact, I was shocked, appalled and outraged when I first discovered in the mid-1990s that Brendan Smyth had gone on to abuse others. I assumed and trusted that when Bishop McKiernan brought the evidence to the Abbot of Kilnacrott that the Abbot would then have dealt decisively with Brendan Smyth and prevented him from abusing others. With others, I feel betrayed that those who had the authority in the Church to stop Brendan Smyth failed to act on the evidence I gave them. However, I also accept that I was part of an unhelpful culture of deference and silence in society, and the Church, which thankfully is now a thing of the past.

As to other children named in the evidence recorded during the Inquiry process, I had no further involvement in the Inquiry process once I handed over the evidence taken. I trusted that those with the authority to act in relation to Brendan Smyth would treat the evidence seriously and respond appropriately. I had no such authority to act and even by today's guidance from the State I was not the person who had the role of bringing the allegations received to the attention of the civil authorities. I was also acutely aware that I had no authority in Church law in relation to Brendan Smyth or any other aspect of the Inquiry process.

I deeply regret that those with the authority and responsibility to deal appropriately with Brendan Smyth failed to do so, with tragic and painful consequences for those children he so cruelly abused.

Suffice to say this statement didn't satisfy me. It was almost entirely defensive. I had hoped for contrition.

However, a few days later, after some time spent praying at the Lough Derg pilgrimage centre in Donegal, Cardinal Brady finally acknowledged that the families should have been notified and warned.

Speaking to RTÉ's Northern Editor Tommie Gorman, he said:

The events of the last week and indeed the events of thirty-seven years ago featured a lot in my thoughts.

It has brought home to me a new realisation of the enormity of child sexual-abuse and I once again want to apologise to all victims of those who have suffered.

I also realised, too, that in the particular incident in Dundalk, the parents of the victims should have been informed. I regret very much that they weren't and obviously if we were in this situation now, I would insist that they are informed.

The question was posed – if he had his time over again would he insist that his bishop inform the parents?

I would be absolutely certain that this should be done. It would be a matter of insisting that somebody would do it, because the parents have a right to know, and the fact that they weren't informed was a great source of pain and further traumatisation to these children. I wasn't as keenly aware of the need to inform the parents as I am now.

And this time he offered a public apology to me.

> I apologise without hesitation to him. [He said]
> I offered that apology last Christmas. I offered to
> come and see him in person. He wanted a public
> apology, it didn't happen, but I repeat now that I
> publicly apologise to him. I'm sorry that I am not
> doing that personally but I would like to do that
> too at the earliest opportunity.

All of this was a significant development as far as I was concerned. Whatever way you look at it, he was finally accepting some personal responsibility for what had not been done.

Not that he was going to resign. That wasn't on the cards, instead plans were being drawn up for his replacement to be put in place; a coadjutor bishop was to be appointed.

I'm often asked what I think of the Cardinal. My answer might appear complex. I don't think he is the devil incarnate. I don't think that he is fundamentally a bad man. In fact, I suspect he is like most of us, trying to do his best, in whatever circumstances he finds himself in.

But he messed up in 1975. It wasn't enough to pass on the information and not make sure that the children's families were told. The worst example of this is his interview with Cavan Boy. Like me, Cavan Boy was interviewed alone, but, unlike me, his parents were never told. Not a word. Wrong. So wrong. And I can't accept that the man who did this should be the head of the Irish Catholic Church when it is trying to root out clerical abuse from its culture.

And a word about not contacting the gardaí. This I don't blame him for, but I do blame his superior Bishop McKiernan and the Norbertine Order. Whatever Cardinal Brady knew about Smyth's activities in 1975, the Bishop and the Order knew much, much more. This was no ordinary child abuser they were dealing with. They knew he had been a problem for decades. He'd been sent for treatment at least three times and was still at it. Nothing had stopped him. It was easier for them to protect the Church's reputation from scandal than go to the authorities.

* * *

The film went on to win a BAFTA in 2013 for the BBC and the team. When they accepted the honour, they dedicated the victory to all victims of abuse. But its impact was still rolling on for me.

Through the film, I was contacted by a number of others who had been abused by Smyth. Two people stand out: Helen McGonigle, who had been attacked in the 1960s when Smyth was a priest in Rhode Island and, separately, another woman we will call 'Mary', who was abused in Ireland.

Helen and I made contact over Facebook and we became friends before we met up in the US when Martina and I were over on a holiday. By coincidence, Helen lives close to relatives of ours, where we were staying.

A dinner was organised at her home. She had arranged for another abuse victim ('John') and his partner to visit her home, to meet us as well. I think there was more significance in the evening than any of us understood. John had travelled some three hours through the snow that night. I was very anxious myself but Helen greeted us all with a big hug and soon we were talking like old friends, or old comrades. Maybe comrades is the best description because we have all been to war and survived. We are all still in touch.

Another meeting with another of Smyth's victims was more difficult for me. Mary contacted me after she read about how I blamed myself for the death of Stephen. We met at a restaurant in the summer of 2013.

If I had been anxious seeing Helen, I was sick with worry in the run-up to the meeting with Mary. She was one of Smyth's youngest victims. I explained to Martina, as I had many times before, how I felt responsible for these youngsters being abused after the inquiry in 1975. They were children that I had let down.

We were sitting at a table when this petite girl walked towards me and Martina. Her husband behind her was about seven-foot tall. She threw her arms around me and gave me a hug. One of the first things she said to me was, 'Please don't feel guilty for the abuse I suffered.'

She is now only thirty-one. I am fifty-two. I am the same age as her dad. No matter what she says, this is messing with my head. We talked for almost four hours in the restaurant, then for another couple of hours in a bar, then until half three in the morning in a parked car. Sometimes laughing, sometimes crying.

She remembers Smyth blessing her mother's tummy when she was pregnant. Later, her baby brother was born asleep, still-born. She has linked this to her abuse and carries guilt because of it. It is nonsense, just like me blaming myself for Stephen's death is nonsense, but it tells you about the burden that that monster has left us with.

Meanwhile, Belfast Boy and I have become close. Martina and I have holidayed with him at his Donegal home and intend to go again.

We spent a wonderful time in his idyllic cottage overlooking a trout-filled lake. We talked and sang and laughed late into the night. So late, the barbecue wasn't lit until 2 a.m! But the fish we cooked – that day's catch – was all the finer for it. The sun was up in the East when we went to bed.

I've seen him with his band, strutting his stuff, just in heaven, brilliant! An amazing bloke. I picture him now, playing his fiddle and his tin whistle with explosive energy and wondrous skill in venues around Ireland; I see a survivor. Wounded, scarred but fighting yet.

* * *

My faith has gone. Entirely. That is my faith in the Catholic institution. I still have a deep sense of God and even prayer, but I have no belief in the structures of the Catholic Church that I was brought up with. Martina feels the same. This is no indictment of individual priests or nuns, or any religious, but I have come to believe that God isn't a manager; he's not the boss man presiding over an earthly organisation of clerical bureaucrats.

No. He's a spiritual incarnation of goodness and truth and help. That's my God. He's not about basilicas and cathedrals, and hierarchy, and power and control, which is what the Catholic Church has been about for too long. I do like the sound of Pope Francis, though. He is a man that, I think, I could talk to about my God.

I have faith in people. Like all my friends and family who have helped us over the years. People like Gill and Tony Tohill. They had their own tragedy when their son Liam died suddenly of a massive stroke. I hope we helped them cope with their grief, but I know we could never have done as much for them as they had done for us when Stephen died.

I often wonder how things have affected my father over the years. I know he has been there for me throughout the years and carried his own guilt. The last thing that I want is for him to lose his faith, for which he has lived his life. He respects my views on religion as I respect his.

I see now that he and my mother had been through an awful shocking time. He's pushing ninety-one now, but we have some of our best chats when we meet. He's more open to talking about what happened today than he ever was then.

He blames himself; I know that. He's told me he should have protected me and not let Smyth into the house. The truth is that people like Smyth are experts at getting people's trust. Daddy and Mammy didn't stand a chance.

I speak to him on the phone regularly and see him as often as possible. I get home to Dundalk several times a year. It's a changed place. The signs of the economic devastation after the financial collapse are there to be seen in the ghost estates and the for-sale signs and empty shops.

But there are other changes too. There is a far greater diversity of people, Eastern Europeans and Africans. I was showing pictures of a recent St Patrick's Day parade in the town to a friend of mine in England, who happens to be of Caribbean heritage. He thought, for an instant, that he'd stumbled on the Notting Hill Carnival. I explained that these are some of the faces that make up new, modern Ireland. All change. And change can be a good thing; that's one thing I am certain about.

It had been a momentous time. I had taken control over what had happened to me; I had taken control of my life. Now, maybe for the first time in decades, I was in charge – not the outside world, not Smyth, not the Church – just me, and Martina. We had come around the mountain and as a couple were in a new place. We are there still, in a better place, looking to the future.

Everything that I was worried about, what people thought about me, I now realise I had nothing to worry about. I have felt the weight coming off my shoulders. I am getting better.

It's been eleven years since we lost Stephen. It is said that time heals, but I can't say that's true. Yes, we have learned to live with it. Not a day goes by that we don't think about him though. We miss him dearly.

We have good foundations to do some rebuilding on. Niall and Sara have had another child. Baby Alanna came along on 11 January 2013. She is adorable and the first Boland girl, since Eilish, in forty-eight years.

They live close by so we see lots of them. Doting grandparents. I want to play a major role in the lives of Frankie and Alanna, but I won't interfere in the way they are being brought up because that's Niall and Sara's department. I'll be watching, though.

I'm so glad things have worked out for Niall. I was worried for him. Sara is a great girl and they're engaged to be married. That will be a proper celebration. I know they will have a great life together.

For my own part, I don't know if I am ever going to fully recover from what I have been through. I am not sure that's possible. Ask Martina. She will tell you that she, that both of us, have lost twenty years that will never come back. We will carry on and I am still getting stronger, but I don't think there are ever happy endings to stories about child abuse. Can't be. But we will survive it.

Acknowledgements

Since 1975 a number of people have had influence and impact on my life. I would like to thank them for their help and support throughout the years.

My wife Martina and sons Stephen and Niall, for their love and understanding. I know there were difficult times for them too.

My father Frank and mother Anna; my sisters and their husbands: Anne and Jimmy, Moira and David, Eilish and Trevor; my nieces and nephews: Conor, Orlagh, David, Lisa and Hannah, who were all there when I needed a shoulder to lean on.

I thank Oliver McShane for doing the decent thing back then and for supporting me through my long court battle. He is truly an amazing friend; Garda Sgt Larry Withrow for his professionalism, sensitivity and patience while recording my lengthy statement at Dundalk Garda Station in 1994; my solicitor Paul Horan in Galway, Brian Coady in Navan, senior counsel Henry O'Burke and the entire legal team who worked tirelessly through a very difficult and complex court case; Ebhard O'Callaghan, R.I.P., my counsellor for almost twenty years, a very kind, gentle and thoughtful man; Marie McCormack, also a victim of Smyth. She was always at the end of the phone when I needed support; lifelong friends, Tony and Gill Tohill and Seán and Brigid Whelan, who helped my family settle in England. They were there to support and comfort us through our most difficult times and, in particular, following the death of our son Stephen; Liam Reilly of Bagatelle, who kindly allowed me to use the lyrics from 'Trump Card' and 'Second Violin'. Both songs are of significant meaning to me. Thank you, Dice.

I would also like to thank: the BBC team: Darragh MacIntyre, Alison Millar, Sam Collyns, Louise Liddy and Séamus McCracken for the BAFTA award-winning documentary *The Shame of the Catholic Church* (*This World*), exposing the Church's cover-up of child sexual abuse perpetrated by paedophile priests; Michael O'Brien and his team at O'Brien Press for trusting me and having faith in my story; Ebury Press, my UK publisher; my good friend Belfast Boy and all his family; and my gratitude goes to my friend Darragh MacIntyre for his encouragement and expertise when putting my story into words.

Happy days on holiday at Greenore, just fifteen miles from home.

*Brendan aged twelve, posing at Bryne's
photographers after his confirmation.*

Family photo taken in 2001. Martina, Brendan,
Niall (13) and Stephen (15).

Brendan with Darragh MacIntyre, today.

Brendan Boland was born in 1961 into a strong Catholic family. In 1975, at the age of fourteen, Brendan was questioned by a secret canonical inquiry and he bore witness to how he and others were being sexually abused by Father Brendan Smyth. Brendan believed that Fr Smyth would be dealt with and would no longer have access to children. This transpired not to be the case. In 1991 Fr Brendan Smyth was arrested, and in 1994 he was jailed for the first time. He was eventually convicted of dozens of offences against many children over a forty-year period. Brendan heard of this news while living in England and his life was turned upside down yet again.

In 1983 Brendan had married his long-term sweetheart, Martina, and had moved to England in search of work. In 1991 he found work with News International, and he is still employed there today, as an engineer. Brendan and Martina had two sons, Stephen and Niall. Brendan lives in Essex, England.

Darragh MacIntyre is an award-winning investigative reporter and the author of *Conversations – Snapshots of Modern Irish Life*. He was the reporter and the presenter of the BAFTA award-winning BBC programme, *The Shame of the Catholic Church*, broadcast in May 2012. Originally from Celbridge, County Kildare, Darragh now lives in Belfast.